THE POWER OF EVOLVED LEADERSHIP

THE POWER OF
EVOLVED
LEADERSHIP

INSPIRE TOP PERFORMANCE
BY FOSTERING INCLUSIVE TEAMS

STEPHEN YOUNG
AND BARBARA HOCKFIELD

Mc
Graw
Hill

NEW YORK   CHICAGO   SAN FRANCISCO   ATHENS   LONDON
MADRID   MEXICO CITY   MILAN   NEW DELHI
SINGAPORE   SYDNEY   TORONTO

1 2 3 4 5 6 7 8 9   LCR   28 27 26 25 24 23

ISBN   978-1-260-01083-1
MHID   1-260-01083-X

e-ISBN   978-1-260-01084-8
e-MHID   1-260-01084-8

McGraw Hill books are available at special quantity discounts to use as premiums and sales promotions or for use in corporate training programs. To contact a representative, please visit the Contact Us pages at www.mhprofessional.com.

McGraw Hill is committed to making our products accessible to all learners. To learn more about the available support and accommodations we offer, please contact us at accessibility@mheducation.com. We also participate in the Access Text Network (www.accesstext.org), and ATN members may submit requests through ATN.

Contents

Acknowledgments

A very warm thank-you to the senior executives who agreed to be interviewed for this book. Their insights and perspectives provided a depth and broad spectrum of leadership viewpoints. Our conversations were rich and even more mind expanding than I could have expected. They have enriched the pages of this book and me as an individual, and my hope is that they will benefit all of you as you journey through the pages of this book. My personal thanks to:

- James Amos, former Commandant, US Marine Corps
- Bob Benmosche, former CEO, AIG
- Mark Bertolini, former CEO, Aetna
- Mike Casey, CEO. Carters
- Ritch Gaiti, former IT Director, Bank of America
- William Gray, former US Congressman and President of the United Negro College Fund
- David Joyce, former President & CEO, GE Aviation
- Dara Khosrowshahi, CEO, Uber
- Spiro Mitrokostas, Owner/Operator, Cooke's
- Mark Pearson, President & CEO, Equitable

- Susan Richards, Educator, Math/Science, Pinole Valley High School, West Contra Costa Unified School District
- Steve Turner, Managing Director, Head of Data Analytics & Marketing Technology, Bank of America
- Jennifer Zatorski, President, Christie's

Throughout their careers, these esteemed leaders have applied their leadership philosophies to achieve business success. None profess to hold the scepter as the definitive source of ideal leadership behavior. Their perspectives are uniquely their own. Their personal practices are featured solely to broaden your perspective for building a customized personal set of best practices that match your developing style as an evolved leader.

Also, thank you Alex Young for providing fresh insight and perspective throughout this process. The panorama of your highly analytical vision has enriched the pages of this book.

Thank you for purchasing this book. We encourage your opinions and feedback on its value for raising your leadership effectiveness.

Special Acknowledgment

Barbara Hockfield is the cofounder and Managing Director of Insight Education Systems, the company behind the development of this book's content and corporate consultation on the topic of unconscious bias globally.

The formation of this project spanned a journey across many arduous, unpaved developmental curves of the creative and research process. As the project reached its stride, three years of the Covid pandemic stepped in with a seeming intent to forestall the process. It was indistinguishable from the plight of Sisyphus. Guiding that boulder forward was Barbara's mental muscle. She directed the team to outmaneuver the obstacles, ensuring the proud outcome of this rich, creative product.

The project encompasses hundreds of hours of dedicated writing, executive interviews, rewriting, content research, rewriting, concept development and testing, more rewriting, focus groups, and more rewriting. Barbara's executive management skills from her impressive Wall Street career became an integral part of our success at each step.

Her insight, intellect, and innovative thinking were cornerstones upon which every paragraph in this book rests.

From inception, through authoring, to the very title itself, this book would never exist without her wisdom, collaboration, and tireless commitment.

Preface

WHAT IS AN EVOLVED LEADER?

A quick historical stroll through the business landscape takes us to the genesis of urban civilization in Mesopotamia, about 3,000 BCE. There was no competitive chase for profit margins. It wasn't about stocks, but stockpiling. Communities had a work culture of collaboration and interdependency. They accumulated commodities, not currency.

As cities arose, class distinctions emerged. It became more apparent who "had" and who "had not." Leapfrogging over the business evolution of the Phoenicians, the Persian Empire, and the Macedonian and the ancient Roman marketplaces gives us a quick look at the agricultural and industrial eras, which witnessed little change in the business infrastructure. Businesses tended to be family-run operations until Alexander Hamilton began the ramping up of true entrepreneurship in the late 1700s with a vision of an industrial nation.

Businesses emerged in various industries: banking, transportation, shipping and freight, agriculture, construction, and textiles.

Albeit the railroads were the genesis of the corporate workplace and a complex managerial structure, it was a new system of layered accountability. The beginning of the twentieth century ushered in a rapid transformation for business with a shift from "mom and pop" to "Inc." These new companies required management to run them and their growing staffs.

Throughout these many stages of career evolution, although much has changed in the products and services provided, change in the culture of the internal workplace has been far more modest. No doubt, environmental safety has made meteoric progress, minimum wages set a standard of compensation, and work hours are now more supportive of physical and mental health. Yet the changes in workplace culture have not realized the same progress. There are still, as was with the railroad workplace at the turn of the twentieth century, ego-filled bosses who expect their underlings to snap to their directives. TGIF is not just an acronym; it's something employees daydream about as the end of the workweek approaches.

What are the skills that make some leaders great and others merely transactional executives?

A central theme in this book is its focus on how leadership behaviors need to evolve from these past practices if we want to motivate, inspire, build loyalty, and enable those with whom we work to perform to their full potential.

This book is meant to spark an evolutionary mission. Workers have been in a business community for about 5,000 years. Although the curve of culture change is rapidly accelerating upward, it may prematurely level off and not continue to ascend reaching the level it ideologically should.

Being a great leader is about creating that type of work environment. It's not merely about being happy and enjoying the workplace;

it must include the practicality of making the business successful and enabling everyone within it to perform to fullest potential. Reaching that plateau could plod along at a snail's pace, or it could take an accelerated path when evolved leadership practices are applied.

What are the skills that make some leaders great and others merely transactional executives? Great leaders are those who become catalysts that enable all those with whom they work to perform to their full potential.

A NEW SET OF BEHAVIORS IS NEEDED

So let's set the stage as we begin the journey. Everything we do in the workplace is done to achieve a series of business outcomes. To be clear, this is not to say that people should pretend—that they should be fake, phony, or manipulative. The idea is to do whatever it takes to be effective as long as it doesn't violate one's core values. And that objective rests on the belief that the scaffolding at the core of great leadership is the ability to motivate, inspire, and get people to live up to their potential.

Leadership messages are particularly powerful when they emanate from those with hierarchical influence.

The term "evolved leader" is, of course, not literal. There will be no spinning of a chrysalis from which you will emerge transformed. This is about an evolved set of behaviors that, in many ways, are no less transcendent than the emergence of the butterfly. It's the shift from obliviousness, or even blindness, to vision.

There is a collective blindness often fueled by good intentions. For the most part, people come to work with good intentions. They want to do a good job and emulate the behaviors that traditionally represent good leadership. Because of these good intentions, there is often a failure to see where our behaviors might fall short.

Most leaders develop their skills by observation of other leaders. This on-the-job training creates a cycle of cultural tradition. People act as they see others act. Even when formal leadership training is provided, its focus tends to be far more along the lines of transactional management training versus true leadership development.

The distinguishing difference between the good manager and the evolved leader might be described as checking the boxes and completing obligatory tasks versus exploring what is often not seen and developing an extraordinarily effective communication ability that gets people to perform to their maximum potential for the organization and themselves.

We will explore the distinguishing characteristics of an evolved leader by breaking down the scaffolding of the four key sectors: *performance, motivation, vision,* and *values* (PMVV). All leadership goals, behaviors, and assessments of one's leadership acumen are defined within these four sectors:

- ▶ **Performance** represents the achievement of a defined set of targeted goals and objectives.
- ▶ **Motivation** encompasses leadership behaviors that create a culture and environment fostering commitment, engagement, motivation, and inspiration.
- ▶ **Vision** sets the trajectory of the business, its evolution, and innovation to achieve long-term success.
- ▶ **Values** establish the ethics and morality of a leader and the shaping of operational culture.

Over the course of my career, I have had the honor to work with many successful corporate leaders. I've also worked with many who were exceedingly substandard. In interesting ways, I learned much from both cohorts about what was effective, how to replicate it, and, conversely, what to avoid.

My awakening of how management styles influence performance was first ignited when I was placed into a matrix reporting structure. I reported to two bosses from different business units. They could not have been more extreme in their management styles; yet each had the power to affect 50 percent of my annual performance review. This became a near potion for schizophrenia!

I would spend an hour in the morning with one boss who was routinely attentive, engaging, supportive, and respectful. It was clear he always had my best interests in mind. That afternoon I would be thrown into the arena with a Hydra. I recall colleagues emerging from his office looking as if they had stepped out of a washing machines' high-speed spin cycle. The contrast in leadership styles could not be overstated.

My curiosity piqued as I analyzed with fine-tuned magnification the extreme behavioral differences in leadership styles. Odd as it may seem, I came to look forward to stepping in and out of these two parallel universes, enjoying this analytical process.

I learned what caused my colleagues to acquiesce and be fearful of challenging anything the boss might advocate and generally being miserable at the thought of coming to work. Oddly, that leader's pernicious leadership style actually got a fair amount of work done—but at what cost?

Turnover ran rampant. Colleagues would regularly undermine one another to ensure they weren't the first to be called to the chopping block. The boss's intimidating style discouraged any risk-taking initiative.

In stark contrast, the other universe was an environment where people spoke their minds freely, comfortably challenged the boss, took initiative, willingly went the extra mile, and were supportive of their colleagues.

Over the years, analyzing the differences in leadership behaviors became a passionate avocation. There were wide ranges of tonal and inflection markers, which, on the surface, would appear indistinguishable. When carefully observed, and an adequate sample base was established, interestingly, those messaging markers became as distinct and reliable as any formal language in interpreting the true meaning of the message.

This platform of "micromessaging" became the basis for my collaboration with Mary Rowe, an MIT professor who first coined the term "micro-inequity," which became the inspiration for my previous book on this topic, *Micromessaging: Why Great Leadership Is Beyond Words.*

Reading someone's subtle micromessages is as close to Mr. Spock's mind melding as it gets to interpreting another's deepest thoughts.

On the most basic level, once you have spent enough time with someone, you are likely to notice when sentiments are off-key and so ask, "What's wrong?" Even with the most minimal skills, when the reply is an indifferent, "Oh, nothing," it's easily detectable that something is plaguing the person—and it's likely something you did that caused it.

The commonplace interpretation of that proverbial "Oh, nothing" is instinctively learned. It would be the anomaly for one not to see and react to it by probing and making an effort to uncover the roots of the unspoken truth.

I have spent extensive time and research digging up these communication roots, brushing them clean, and examining the fibers. Without the right tools, those roots lie hidden beneath us, in plain sight.

In some ways, it is a type of portable communications decoding lab. Its valuable application is in uncovering the "poker tells" of communication dynamics that inspire and motivate performance through the signals we send.

In the last decade, our company's process for dissecting leadership behaviors has extended to all levels of management hierarchy, across 35 countries and more than a dozen industries.

As you walk through the pages of this book, I invite you to apply these strategies and action-based skills to optimize your presence and impact as an evolved leader.

THE POWER OF
EVOLVED
LEADERSHIP

CHAPTER 1

Setting the Stage

There seem to be more new books on leadership than "foodie fotos" on social media. There is a flood of new images; yet few are drawn to digest them all. This book seeks to open *fresh* windows of leadership vision and behavior. It reaches beyond bland pablum and platitudes and cuts new paths of leadership behavior.

As we begin this book, let me reference the end. In the epilogue we will explore whether human leaders will be needed at all! The advent and future application of AI has the potential to restructure everything in ways that may be unrecognizable. Until that day, the focus of this book explores the ways humans can optimize their leadership effectiveness now and into the future.

As one who has worked closely with C-suite executives in the largest commercial bank in the United States, I developed a great deal of frustration watching them, and other colleagues, make critical decisions limited by traditions of preset protocols.

Not unlike soldiers, these leaders marched in lockstep, taking direction from those with more stripes. Hierarchy drove the determination of right and wrong. I understood what they were going through—I assimilated much of those practices into my own belief system when I worked in the corporate world. At the time, I felt proud to be a part of the regime, likely due to my esteemed membership in that power club.

But here was the problem: Groundbreaking, innovative thinking beyond a relatively small leeway was all but extinguished, especially if it came from someone outside the inner circle of the anointed.

In this book, we will examine the conscious and unconscious ways language and culture influence the development of an innovative workforce and how mastering these nuances can accelerate the evolution of leadership to rise above the limitations imposed by practicality and protocol—and to move closer toward achieving innovation and competitive ideology.

The decisions we make each day tend to be influenced predominantly by practicality, not ideology. What we wear, how gingerly we express disagreement, whose jokes we laugh at, and how we respond to a broad spectrum of social and office politics are actions taken with careful consideration to winning acceptance and approval from those with whom we live and work. Gauging how much to push back against the prevailing culture hinges on the political power (hierarchical or otherwise) of those we push.

Control of the knobs and switches in the game of workplace power dynamics is often won through the dynamics of behavioral perception and social skills, as well as natural instinct. Those possessing higher levels of skill and perception are more likely to find themselves at the top of the leaderboard.

Psychologist Abraham Maslow had it right. Fear and survival are among the most powerful motivating forces.

In 1943, Abraham Maslow published his paper, "A Theory of Human Motivation." It established a theory that remains a central pillar of psychological quality of life.

Hierarchical power in the workplace is the path to achieve that critical sense of safety and security that Maslow believed people crave.

In *The Wizard of Oz*, Dorothy needed the good witch Glinda to reveal that she had the power all along to get back home. (I can't believe that "witch" withheld that critical information to herself for so long!) In the workplace, it is often the reverse.

People deceive themselves into believing they have more power than they actually do. Once they get burned attempting to usurp the boss's authority, they quickly learn the silent rules of office politics and how the game must be played—at least today.

Those of us who have taken a naïve, ideological misstep in a traditional organization know how quickly that overstepping can get the carpet pulled from under our feet. The world didn't need to wait until 1943 to hear it from Maslow. Our awareness of the need to filter our actions through fear and survival in every decision we make is instinctive. You just need to quickly learn how it uniquely works where you are.

IDEOLOGY VERSUS PRACTICALITY

Ideology and practicality are competing motivational forces. The art of balancing them well is central to becoming the evolved architects of tomorrow's leadership. In order to make meaningful advancements toward workplace ideology, we must begin to change the existing cultural soil to enable more rapid realization.

Ideology and its evil twin, practicality, are the ever-present devil and angel voices in our heads. Ideology, or the true north of leadership behavior, is what will unbind the old-world strings that tie people down to politically-laden thinking and behavior.

To be clear, we are not suggesting that practicality is pure evil. Practicality is the necessary compromise when ideology prevents one from making progress. The real world demands that we cannot always practice the ideal. We must compromise in an artful balance of both.

One voice tells us what we should do if decisions are being made in an unfettered workplace—with no fear of needing to pander to higher practicality or social conditions. The other voice seeks to ensure our safety, guiding us away from the perils of not playing the game by the rules set by those in power.

Ideology and its evil twin, practicality, are the ever-present devil and angel voices in our heads.

An indelible memory of the devil and angel bumping heads was when I presented to the CEO and C-suite of a multinational food/snack manufacturer. We had completed three pilot review seminars across several departments within the company to more than 200 employees. The feedback from those sessions was consistently high, and the senior leadership team was asked to review the program and sanction a broad-scale rollout. The day for that meeting finally arrived. Early in the presentation, I asked the executive team members what they felt were the most important attributes of a great leader.

Surprisingly, it seemed all heads turned in deference toward the CEO, who then stood and pontificated his perspective. He elaborated on the importance of understanding the business, knowing your people, having challenging targets and objectives, ensuring people get rewarded for doing well, having charisma, and being a great communicator, along with possessing several other requisite skills.

His tone was condescending and carried an air of: *Now that Daddy has told you, I want you children to go out and do as I have instructed.*

He did not mention the three key attributes that are the cornerstone of great leadership—those being the skills to motivate, inspire, and enable others to perform to their potential.

Feeling the shortcoming of his message, I opened the door, just a little too wide, letting the devil twin take the mic. Ever so politely, but very directly, I countered his perspective on leadership. I pointed out that while understanding the business, knowing your people, being a great communicator, and all the other attributes he mentioned are important—they are not central in defining the ultimate objective of what a great leader accomplishes. Great leadership requires having a direct effect on, motivating, inspiring, and enabling others to perform to their potential.

It seemed his team agreed, albeit timidly and silently, heads nodding—until they turned and looked at the CEO. The expression on his face spoke volumes. There were no words, but his thoughts were clear—"How dare you come into my kingdom and attempt to undermine me." I could hear his thoughts, "It's the last time you'll be coming here!"

It was just another example of how silence can be unmistakably palpable.

In an unevolved workplace culture, the practicality devil speaks to us with a voice more intimidating than Darth Vader and more persuasive than a television evangelist. On the other shoulder, the ideology angel is more reminiscent of a Stephen Hawking, who in his twilight had no natural voice at all, yet guided a thinking process of logic, reason, and mind expansion. Which one wins? It is based entirely on who wields the scepter and sets the culture.

Although every thinking person knows there is greater morality from the voice of one's internal idealistic angel, there are some very real dangers to ignoring the caution emanating from that voice of practicality.

In most workplaces, success requires knowing and playing by the unspoken rules of the organization's culture while subtly injecting behaviors of idealism that raise the workplace culture closer, albeit slowly, to the true north of leadership.

My Grandfather's World

Throughout my childhood, I watched my grandfather's self-deprecating posture in public toward his White superiors, and White people in general. He was a renowned deacon for one of the most influential Black churches in the state of Maryland. He was the model of confidence and integrity with a natural idealistic persona of a strong leader. He never pandered while in the safe haven of his church's enclave. In that community, there was no fear of survival; his job stability and income were not in jeopardy.

Outside that setting, his persona shifted radically, influenced by a fear for his safety—of not being able to simply walk the streets without law enforcement intimidation or racial persecution. In his workplace, the focus of his persona shifted yet again from personal safety to job stability, rooted in the same racial issues. His persona shifts were highly predictable social models taking him from a meek deferential persona to a strong community leader, all influenced by the need to survive or the comfort of genuine self-expression.

As I would walk with him through town, it was a no-brainer which of these two inner voices would prevail. It was never a draw. The practicality voice would always wipe the floor with his ideology counterpart and would take him face down to the canvas, often rendering my naturally glib grandfather unable to speak at all.

Once he passed back through the portal of the "upside down" into his church's safe haven, his persona shifted back. Practicality no longer had power over his decision-making. The idealism of his religious responsibilities transcended, and the strong leader within vibrantly reemerged.

To evolve, the brave must always set their sights on the ideological pursuit, while keeping a careful eye on the possible landmines and potholes that can derail their quest.

Language and Culture

Tolerances of workplace ideology, or the freedom to challenge, vary widely across industries and cultures. The language itself varies based on the need for clarification and understanding.

The Inuit are said to have over 20 words for "snow" as a reflection of their environment. For them, that fluffy white stuff is ubiquitous, and so much of their existence reflects its pervasiveness. They have developed a deeper level of perception about snow as it relates to the subtleties of their surroundings. Language morphs to reflect the environment it supports. Language morphing is integral in the culture of industries, as well.

There is the language of industry and even languages by industry. People in the tech industry tend to be less socially effusive than those in the sports world. Those in the world of theater make others appear socially comatose by comparison. Thespians are "on" 24/7—waiting ever patiently for the klieg lights to shine so they can take over the scene. In fact, many of them don't even wait for the lights. They just step in and take control.

In the tech world, there is no pressing need to make a computer smile or like you to get the work done. In sales and marketing, mastering the language of emotion and persuasion is at the epicenter of success.

Is industry language a case of the chicken or the egg? Is a person drawn to an industry based on its language culture, or does one adapt and assimilate into that industry's existing language culture in order to succeed?

What is indisputable is the need to match organizational language and assimilate within an organization's culture. The working parts of organizational language incorporate more than simple terms alone. They are distinguished by the micromessages of tone, nuance, inflection, inference, facial expressions, eye contact, syntax, and a myriad of other indicators. When mastered well, these become the keys that unlock and accelerate one's leadership trajectory.

A member of the executive suite often projects an aura of stature that is easily distinguishable from that of middle managers within that company. Even mildly observant outsiders could have a random encounter with each, and there would be little doubt they'd be able to identify the different positions in the hierarchy.

There are clear distinctions of cultural language across disciplines, as well. HR has a communication and operational culture that is different from that in legal. Sales culture differs from that of manufacturing, while marketing's culture is uniquely different from that of finance.

These cultural language distinctions are not relegated to business groups alone. Cultural language can be hierarchical, as well. Power sets culture. A senior executive who heads a business group has the power to cascade a communication and interaction style that sets the tone for how all others within that group behave.

To be effective, one cannot be oblivious to these varying cultural frameworks. One's effectiveness often hinges on the ability to tune in and speak the language of the community within which the person operates.

The Challenge of Culture Change

Evolved leaders don't allow their personal communication preferences to dictate how others can safely express ideas and challenges. Actively look for the differences in communication styles within your team and openly acknowledge them. Make clear statements of their value and your appreciation of the differences. By spotlighting these, you foster a culture that has no uniform or required method of communicating to which others are expected to adhere—as long as they are productive and move the business forward.

WHAT IS LEADERSHIP?

Commonly used business terms are often left ill-defined. What exactly is a "good team player"—what does the term "to empathize" mean? Can you clearly define what it looks like to have "charisma"? Does "integrity" simply mean that one never lies, and since we all do, sometimes, does that mean no one has it? For a person to be "transparent," does he or she really have to tell you everything? The everyday list of common business terms remains woefully ill-defined. But the fog of their definitions is routinely dismissed, and we live in an amorphous interpretation of their meaning.

This book seeks to provide the clarity that enables us to establish both uniformity and consistency in understanding the business terms we use. It seems appropriate that we bring clarity to these ill-defined terms by first defining the term "leadership" itself.

I recently asked a middle manager to define the term "leadership." Not "good leadership" or "weak leadership," but the intrinsic meaning of the word itself. He found it difficult without giving examples of how to do it well or poorly.

After a long pause, his description went directly to the people component—"It's the people in power within an organization," he said. If this were true, then leadership would be defined simply by titles and names. That would be a thin and quite shallow definition for something as dynamic and complex as leadership.

A CHALLENGE: DEFINE LEADERSHIP

Take a pause. Give careful thought to how you would define leadership. Here's your challenge: Imagine someone approaches you. This person has no understanding of corporate culture or the business lexicon and asks you to define the term.

Define "leadership" for that person in a way that is clear and actionable. Give it a whirl—I'll wait!

So let's move from the ill-defined to the explicitly clear. The definition we offer defines "leadership" as a sociological construct reaching across four discrete skill sectors, which I refer to as the PMV Leadership Model (Figure 1.1):

1. Performance
2. Motivation
3. Vision
4. Values

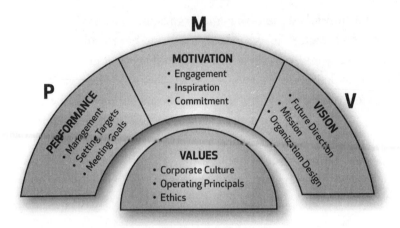

FIGURE 1.1   PMV Leadership Model (Illustration: Jet Jakab)

1. Performance

The Performance sector includes the completion or accomplishment of tasks against established goals and targets. In other words—"getting the business done." Performance is about meeting quotas, hitting revenue targets, staffing, and attaining other measurable objectives. This sector is largely transactional.

This sector of leadership is what is traditionally used in defining the role of a manager. As long as products and services are generating profit margins that meet or exceed performance expectations, that leader (manager) will receive excellent performance reviews.

In my conversation with Steve Turner, managing director, head of Data Analytics & Marketing Technology, Bank of America, he shared that "an effective functional leader empowers a team to be focused on outcomes versus tasks." Actions are important but outcomes define business success.

Although the Evolved Leader model rests on four pillars: Performance, Motivation, Vision, and Values, they are not all equal. Performance triumphs over the others. While one cannot be an admired and evolved leader without all four skill sectors operating at peak levels, without meeting performance standards, a business cannot be sustained.

A company can have the best people, motivate them within an efficient operating culture, have a well-developed plan and vision, and operate with the highest set of values, but if after doing all these processes well, its balance sheet is filled with red ink, its doors will be forced to close.

> An effective functional leader empowers a team
> to be focused on outcomes versus tasks.
> —Steve Turner, managing director, head of
> Data Analytics & Marketing Technology, Bank of America

This Performance sector of leadership is largely built upon a scaffolding of checklists. There is an interdependency between accomplishing the performance requirements and the motivation that enables a team to hit those targets.

The Motivation sector has the greatest influence on enabling the performance elements to be achieved.

2. Motivation

The Motivation sector comprises a broader set of more complex analytical and motivational skills. The focus here is less on the completion of discrete tasks and more on building commitment, engagement, loyalty, and a desire to succeed. One who is skilled in this sector enables others to perform to their potential.

The late Bill Gray was one of the biggest personalities I've known, both physically and in persona. His powerful communication style dominated the room whether giving a sermon at his world renowned Bright Hope Baptist Church in Philadelphia, or speaking as a member of the US House of Representatives over the six terms he served.

Our meeting years ago in his Capitol Hill office was no exception. His experience as a leader spanned from US congressman to president of the United Negro College Fund (UNCF). He dedicated his life to inspiring and motivating people to continually explore new areas of personal growth.

He held the belief that people can never become what they are not exposed to.

This belief was a key factor in his decision to lead the UNCF. In discussing one of the education strategies he was building and how others, who were not a part of his efforts, could support his vision, he passionately said, "Your job, and the job of every person with the power and influence to do so, is to remove the barriers, physical and mental, that keep people from moving beyond the reach of their arms."

He lived by the belief that the greatest leaders are those who develop *new* great leaders. In that process, we are all teachers and learners along that journey.

> Your job, and the job of every person with
> the power and influence to do so, is to remove
> the barriers, physical and mental, that keep people
> from moving beyond the reach of their arms.
> —William Gray, former US congressman and president of the UNCF

This book will focus the lion's share of its content on the Motivation sector of the PMV Leadership Model. This is not to minimize the importance of the other three sectors (performance, vision, and values), but it is the skill of motivation that inspires and enables others to perform to their potential that fuels achievement in the other three sectors.

3. Vision

The Vision sector takes a step above the operational aspects of leadership. Vision looks beyond the current state. It identifies the organization's future direction and provides guidance to ensure continuous growth toward that mission. The Vision sector depends heavily on the activities that comprise the Motivation sector. One can't develop a vision without a strong platform of motivation.

I can't think of anyone who exemplified this more than the visionary icon Bob Benmosche, former CEO of AIG, one of the largest insurance companies in the world. Benmosche was appointed CEO by the US Department of the Treasury and the AIG board of directors to lead the turnaround of AIG during the global financial crisis of 2009. The company received the largest financial bailout in history—$182 billion. It was the classic "too big to fail" company.

Benmosche was selected due to his extraordinary skills at shaping the vision and future direction of a company. He strongly believed that skilled leadership behavior was the cornerstone that would bring the company back from the brink of disaster—and it did! Benmosche's leadership not only brought AIG back to profitability but enabled the company to repay the government loan, as well as an additional $22 billion in interest to the US Treasury.

Our firm was proud to be a part of honing the leadership skills for AIG's transformation. We spent many hours together, in flight, traveling to various AIG locations, building these skills at all the company's regional leadership forums.

According to Benmosche, "Managers drive the activities of a business. Leaders shape the trajectory of its future direction and convey why that is the right path and what is required to reach it." Bob wasn't just able to see the curve ahead. He had the unique ability to see around it and inspire those near him to follow.

> Managers drive the activities of a business. Leaders shape the trajectory of its future direction and convey why that is the right path and what is required to reach it.
> —Bob Benmosche, former CEO, AIG

How is vision achieved? The challenge in developing a business vision is needing to see what is not yet seen in our present state. Begin the process by releasing all constraints surrounding the proverbial "We can't do this because . . . ." Allow your creativity to break its restraints by first assuming that budget is not an issue. Assume there are no limitations on staffing or resources. Assume technology can do anything you can imagine. Ask yourself what path your industry has taken over the past decade and plot a new course that expands beyond that trend. Accept that truisms might not be true and prohibitions do not exist.

The visionary doesn't focus simply on better. The visionary breaks through that boundary and focuses on being the virtuoso who creates innovative outcomes that inspire others to redirect their paths and follow.

4. Values

The Values sector involves ethics in a wide array of applications. As an employee, you need to determine, "Is the company I work for an ethical organization? Is its core business something about which I can be proud? Does it foster practices of integrity within, and externally, with clients and the products and services it provides? Is the work here meaningful? Does the environment create a culture that fosters admiration and respect of the business itself?"

The Values sector is the most subjective and, therefore, the most difficult to qualify and quantify. Ethics sits squarely at its epicenter.

Ethics has been a guiding force for all societies from the beginning of humankind. Determining what is right and wrong, or good versus evil, can be a great unifier or cut a great swath of divisiveness. Our newsfeeds represent this every day.

Ethics are universally subjective by their nature. Even horrendous acts such as abuse, theft, and even murder can be justified through a particular culture's filters of ethics. After all, one person's freedom fighter is another person's terrorist.

Imagine having the opportunity to travel back in history to November 9, 1938, at the Kristallnacht movement when the first 91 Jews of the Holocaust were killed. It's been asked many times, if one had the opportunity to assassinate Adolf Hitler at that time, would this preemptive strike to prevent the Holocaust be ethical—or is murder fundamentally wrong?

George Washington is heralded throughout US history as one of the country's greatest leaders. The opinions of the indigenous people of North America, however, would not likely align with that perspective. These are ethical questions of personal values.

Scholars have mapped ethics into two analytical channels; teleology and deontology. Teleology focuses on the rightness or wrongness of an action by analyzing its consequences. It determines if something is right or wrong based on the outcome or results. In other words, the ends justify the means.

Deontology focuses on the rightness or wrongness of an action, in a vacuum, without any other consideration. In other words, it is simply flat-out right or wrong, regardless of any potential benefit.

These dual channels of ethics apply directly to assessing the quality of a leader in the area of subjective decision-making. Virtually every decision a leader makes can be assessed in different ways, based on one's personal values.

In our personal lives, imagine a child asking a parent, "Mom, is it wrong for me to do this . . . ?" And the mother responds, "Well, tell me how it works out for you at the back end, and I'll let you know." This would be preposterous guidance for determining ethical behavior.

In truth, pretty much all our decisions about social behavior are put through this evolving filter known as "presentism."

The concept of presentism is the process of judging the behaviors of the past using a current-day overlay of standards. It is the stuff that "cancel culture" is made of.

As a child, I didn't mind seeing the iconic Uncle Ben on that rice box. Over the years, my perspective slowly shifted. I developed a growing disdain for that representation as a racial stereotype. It was presentism that made me wag my finger at Mars, Quaker Oats, and other product perpetrators for being so racially tone deaf. Would it have been considered ethically wrong at the time, nearly a century ago, in 1942? Clearly, I was using current-day standards to judge the behaviors of the distant past.

There are certain applications of presentism as a mechanism for judgment that are appropriate. These involve acts of extreme degradation, malice of forethought, and a violation of even those ethical standards that were in place at the time, albeit not rigorously enforced. The United Kingdom knew in 1833 that slavery was morally wrong and acted then to abolish it. Laws were in place to make sexual coercion illegal a century before it became universally verboten. The most heinous despot of all, King Leopold, whose reign of imperial power led to the massacre of more than 10 million people, would not be given a pass under *any* filter. Mass murder was an act of moral barbarism even in the early 1800s.

> **The concept of presentism is the process of judging the behaviors of the past using a current-day overlay of standards.**

These are just some examples of how the Values sector of leadership is also a moving and amorphous yardstick of judgment. And it is not time alone that has the power to shift our perspective on ethics and values.

Some look at whether a company pays equitable wages to its employees at all levels, among countless other ethical filters to judge the worthiness of a company's values—and choose to work for the company, or not, based on this assessment.

This book does not pass judgment on these values nor offer guidance on how to shape them. This commentary on ethics and values is purely intended to delineate the four distinct sectors that define the structure of leadership. Use these filters of values and ethics in determining the companies you will align yourself with and build your career.

CONNECTING THE SECTORS

Juggling the four sectors of leadership is a skill that gets tested, routinely. Sometimes the juggling is easy. Other times, if not well prepared, fate may toss you a greaseball, causing all the others to become tainted, difficult to handle, and tumble to the ground.

Understanding the PMV Leadership Model and its interdependent sectors can help you keep all the proverbial balls in the air. Never stop honing these skills toward leadership excellence.

As the leader, have you ensured that employees fully understand the ways in which they fit into the four sectors of this model?

- Do they clearly understand how their *performance* will be measured in both numerical and behavioral assessments?
- Do they recognize and appreciate the ways in which you *motivate* and inspire their commitment, loyalty, and engagement?
- Do they understand the company's *vision* and how they are expected to actualize it?
- Do they have a sense of pride in the operating principles of the company's *values*?

The PMV Leadership Model visually presents a connected arch linking three of the four sectors: Performance, Motivation, and Vision. These are associated with but not actually connected to the Values sector. This suggests that great leadership can be achieved with high proficiency in three core sectors. The values the leader demonstrates are subjective through the observer's lens.

For example, you cannot be a great leader if you have failed to make performance criteria clear and equitable across the team. This would be true in any culture or any industry. The same holds true for the Motivation sector. If you are unable to generate a sense of commitment, engagement, and motivation, you are not a great leader.

This is certainly true for the Vision sector, as well. If you fail to set the trajectory of where the organization is going and how others will get there, it disqualifies you from being a great leader.

Again, this triad of achievement is necessary to attain great leadership across all industries globally.

The Values sector is an island. It is a subjective set of beliefs and personal values that are not necessarily universal, nor a criterion for great leadership. One's personal values may be at odds with those demonstrated by leadership. This divergence in viewpoints does not necessarily impact great leadership. Someone's values can be totally different from yours, but this does not mean the person is not a great leader. It's all about how much importance you place on the alignment of your values with the company's corporate values that determines whether this is a culture you wish to follow and be a part of.

The company's operating principles and values define whether that environment is the right leadership culture for the employee. When there is core conflict between the corporate values and the individual's personal values, it is a clarion call that it is likely not the right mutual fit.

Examining this dissonance should be pursued from both directions. Leaders need to uncover whether an employee subscribes to the company's operating principles and values. Where these diverge, the evolved leader confronts the employee directly to assess whether the employee can fully commit to the company's mission. Conversely, employees should do the same. If working at a company makes one feel compromised or morally uncomfortable in supporting the company's mission and culture, it may be time to look elsewhere and find a better fit.

TRANSFORMATIONAL VERSUS EVOLVED LEADERSHIP

What is the difference between transformational leadership and evolved leadership? These two perspectives on leadership are very similar. Transformational leadership is a leadership approach that causes change in professional behavior. It creates valuable and positive change, with the end goal of developing followers into leaders. The evolved leadership approach is less of an "approach" and more of an embracing and even an absorption of idealistic and practical facilitation in motivating and inspiring others to perform to their potential.

In simple terms, transformational leaders follow a learned process, while evolved leaders change their fundamental DNA. In a theatrical metaphor, transformational leaders memorize the script and play the part admirably. Evolved leaders are more like the method actor who becomes the role. They are not acting the role; they become the role, woven into the fabric of their daily interactions. Your role as an evolved leader is to optimize organizational culture through these four PMV sectors to drive commitment, engagement, and peak performance for all those with whom you work.

LEADERS SET THE CULTURE

At the highest level, the company's broader culture platform is set by the CEO and cascaded through the company by C-suite executives and their senior teams. In general, this is how corporate culture is propagated.

To understand the power senior executives have on shaping culture, I interviewed leaders across a broad spectrum of industries to uncover how they consciously, or otherwise, create the culture they envision for success. They shared some of their unique leadership techniques, many of which got them to their seats of power and influence.

One leader, Dara Khosrowshahi, the CEO of Uber, talked with me about the importance of distinguishing the difference between leadership and management: "I really look for people who have demonstrated the ability to build teams and what I call 'followership.'" He continued, "Management is contractual and transactional. Leadership is not. It is 'followership-based'—and that is having influence without authority. I look for people who demonstrate the ability to win the hearts and minds of their teams. I tell my managers I want them to aspire to those qualities of leadership."

One particularly interesting pearl from Khosrowshahi was his perspective on "influence without authority." Great leaders, at any level, develop the skill to influence the performance of others without needing hierarchical power to do so. Being a great leader is not about having a title. It's about having the ability to influence the thinking, creativity, and performance of others.

All the successful leaders interviewed for this book applied the fundamental techniques one might expect, but what you'll find particularly illuminating are the many revelations on how they cut new paths toward the evolved leader of the future.

One strikingly consistent message resonating across all the interviews was understanding the practical need to distinguish innovative and visionary thinking from what others might regard as eccentric, or even wacky. It is the skill of balancing perceived risk.

> Leadership is "followership-based"—and that is having influence without authority. I look for people who demonstrate the ability to build teams, winning their hearts and minds.
> —Dara Khosrowshahi, CEO, Uber

One CEO told me about an idea he never shared with his team or board of directors because they would certainly consider it far too crazy. His idea was the complete elimination of the C-suite structure altogether. He imagined replacing it with a new model of congressional-like committees. These committees would be made up of employees who were top performers, had a proven set of skills, and had different perspectives from one another, as well as contrary attitudes regarding risk taking.

Initially, his idea struck me, yes, as a bit wacky, but as it steeped with me over time, I've come to believe it has strong merit. This became a catalyst that ignited expanded thinking of my own and opened the door to the creation of WAID, the WebSphere of Autogenous Interdependencies—a leadership model of the future.

This will be explored later in the Epilogue when we examine the trajectory of our leadership evolution as we hurdle through the twenty-first century and beyond. (And no, he has still not shared the idea with his board.)

As explored earlier, Ideology represents our vision of a perfect process for maximum impact. Practicality takes into consideration risks, resistance, and the wisdom of sacrificing what may be ideal in order to get things done. Interestingly, this also relates to teleological and deontological ethics. The art here is in the balancing of both.

This is a central theme throughout the book that recognizes the inextricable link between doing the right thing (ideology) and getting things done (practicality).

The book's message addresses the value for leaders to shift from the comfort of a safe haven (the way it's done here), to artfully evolve into building a team or entire organization that embraces a culture of ideological practicality.

We will frequently espouse controversial positions and challenge longstanding status quo business principles. These pages seek to build the skills to inspire those around us to transcend cultural convention, protocols, and past practices—and become an evolved leader.

WHO IS THIS BOOK IS FOR?

There are many skills unique to great leadership. They share common threads that cross boundaries, industries, and cultures, and no one can achieve greatness without mastering them. They transcend the unique demands of hierarchical level. Similar to great parenting where attentiveness, respect, support, and other skills are common across all families and cultures, so too are there common skill requirements that lay the foundation for great leadership.

Whether you are a senior executive of a multinational corporation, a leader in a midsize local business, or a manager, or you aspire to a leadership role in any type of organization, the messages in this book are designed to enable you to maximize the three cornerstone skills of great leadership: the ability to motivate, inspire, and enable others to perform to their potential. There is nothing more important than these attributes in defining what great leadership is all about.

Some hold the belief that the ability to generate high levels of revenue is an important indicator of achieving great leadership. *It is not!* Generating revenue merely makes one a highly valued individual contributor. In the world of sports, it is well established that individual achievement does not equate to being a team leader. Players who have the ability to motivate their teammates, build their spirits, encourage their commitment and loyalty, and unify their collective skills are the ones who demonstrate great leadership. They make the whole greater than the sum of its parts.

There is a dichotomy in how this actually plays out. Some team sports require interplay among its team members, as with soccer, football, basketball, and others. Here, interplay is critical. Other sports simply represent a group of individual contributors where this symbiosis is not critical. Even at the Olympic level, ski teams, martial arts teams, tennis teams, and fencing teams are all teams of singularity. Although called a team, the team members all compete as individuals, and their success does not depend on the other members of the team.

In the corporate world, an overwhelming majority of corporate ecosystems depend on interdependent and collaborative high performance. The construct of team singularity—operating in isolation for success—rarely exists in business cultures. In these settings, there is always the need to motivate, inspire, and enable others to live up to their potential as a requirement for great leadership—whether done internally with other team members or externally with clients and customers.

The concepts shared in this book will build your skills to achieve optimum leadership success. If you have the responsibility for managing others or anticipate rising to that level, the skills imparted in this book are designed for you.

CHAPTER 2

Leadership's Natural Selection

Humankind has evolved over millions of years. The earliest record of the species, *Homo habilis*, goes back 2.3 million years. Since that time, our species has undergone many dramatic transformations and spawned countless cultures and societies.

It's well established that the last hundred years, which represent about 0.000025 percent of our timeline, have seen more progress than the previous 99+ percent. The critical question is: What's next, and where do we fit in on that ever-changing and unpredictable evolutionary curve of change? Even more importantly, how can we influence its direction?

Yet when we look at how we select our leaders, remarkably, that sharp evolutionary trajectory has not shared the same rapid progress. We subconsciously continue to choose leaders using many of the same measures of selection as our Neanderthal ancestors. We simply find new terms to define leadership to justify our antiquated criteria and social cues for selection.

In the wild, alpha dogs do not have corner offices or executive assistants, but that deficit has never impaired their ability to reign supreme. As the alpha loses power, there are a number of younger challengers waiting in the wings to fight for the position. In the animal world, this succession planning exercise can be bloody. Fortunately, when the corporate alpha is succeeded, it is far more civilized, but the process operates with comparable initiation.

When the performance of the alpha begins to falter, the successor need not have sharp teeth but, instead, a sharp tongue and mind, along with a proven track record of success. When removed from power, the CEO who weakens or falters often departs with a hefty golden parachute severance package, unlike their animal alpha counterparts who end their reign, literally, belly up. On the front end, however, the ways alpha dogs achieved their indomitable alpha positions are remarkably similar to how humans selected—and still select—leaders.

Neanderthal humans selected leaders using a nearly indistinguishable set of criteria. The biggest, strongest, and most cunning males fought for the leadership role, with one rising above his competitors to take the seat of power. This structure of iron-fisted dominance and control created a culture of "yes-men" underlings. Subordinates followed the boss's bidding, knowing failure to comply could result in their peril and relegate them to the heap of the vanquished.

In our species' evolutionary past, as well as that of many other species, there always came a time when the leader showed signs of weakness and some ambitious upstart would nip at the leader's heels. That challenge was met head on. There was ripping of fur, crashing of antlers, drawing of swords, and an ultimate fight to the death.

The intentions and outcomes were the same. Either the challenger would unseat the incumbent, or the leader would triumph and retain dominance.

For animals and humans, this has been a logical and essential process for natural selection and survival. The community needed the leader who was best equipped to ensure the group's survival. By modeling the cunning behavior and survival skills of the alpha, others learned and adopted techniques for the tribe's protection and survival. This selection model continues for animals and, as we'll see, has only moderately altered for humans.

Although humans are superior to other animals in intellect and wisdom (well mostly), we unwisely, and illogically, hold fast to some of these selection vestiges in the workplace and our political selections. In the United States, most elected presidents have been taller than their rivals. It's unlikely this was merely coincidence. Maybe this was a case where size *did* matter.

Little more than a decade ago, virtually all Fortune 1000 CEOs and C-suite executives were, on average, six feet tall, middle aged, strapping White men.

Their selection was, unconsciously, influenced by deeply rooted Neanderthal predispositions of physical attributes. Although optimal for our survival several millennia ago, oddly, those visual and physical features retain their dominance, fueling many corporate selections even today when such physical attributes are no longer necessary to maintain a leadership position. We must dig down deep and force ourselves to jettison the illogical value of "muscles on the arms" with the wiser choice of "muscles between the ears" to optimize our future survival.

Executive job openings don't list physical attributes among the stated requirements. But if you scan the websites or inquire directly about executive profiles, you'll find virtually no corporate CEOs who have an observable disability, are under five foot six, or are noticeably overweight. The unconscious search for the alpha remains indelibly rooted in our subconscious and manifested in the profiles of the corporate workforce. The thinking part of our brain tells us this is illogical, but the underlying mammalian roots silently creep in, take command, and disrupt our intellect and wisdom.

Selection is not the only manifestation of this outdated and illogical thinking. Fear of challenging the seat of power may be even more endemic to corporate culture. There is an almost axiomatic fear of challenging the boss. Employees may talk among themselves about how a manager's behavior is detrimental to the team, but they usually keep that criticism among themselves.

I remember a conversation in which someone complained about management missing the boat on how to market a new product. He told me his boss had given the team direction on how to position the product with current and prospective clients, but he felt he had a far more effective strategy. I asked the obvious question, "Why don't you tell your boss about your idea?" His answer was predictable. He laughed and said, "Are you kidding? I can't tell my boss that! I'd be screwed. He'd be furious with me telling him how to do his job."

It's the classic manifestation of the old "nipping-at-the-heels" of the alpha dog. The suggestion that someone else is better qualified or more knowledgeable is sometimes seen as a threat, and the vestigial reaction awakens and unleashes the attack mode.

People put more effort into being right than seeking truth.

Our intellect often fools us. We convince ourselves that it is smarter to challenge the boss and bring the better idea to the table. Although that may seem wise, there is that silent Neanderthal voice triggering caution: "Don't poke the bear!" Sure, your boss may tell you that it's OK to challenge, and may even appear to be warm and fuzzy, but our caution to challenging his or her dominance is a risk that we take with great trepidation, if we even dare at all.

The reality is that most people desire to be right and feel embarrassed when they're proved wrong. In other words, our instincts make us defensive. We strive to be right over our desire to seek the truth.

Our egos burn hot. They can even be primal raging blazes that scorch the effectiveness of a workplace. Ego and the need to save face can cause us to blur what otherwise may be easily discernible. It is in our nature to resist the embarrassment of being wrong, and the sting of that embarrassment may strike more painfully when it's the leader who admits to not having the right answers. People put more effort into being right than seeking truth. As we'll learn throughout the book, the ego needs to stand down if we are to pursue truth and be an effective leader.

THE NUMBER ONE OBSTACLE TO LEADERSHIP EVOLUTION

I recall an exciting conversation with two professors who attended one of my keynotes at Harvard University. They deeply connected with my message about the future demands of leadership and shared some details about a particular research project they had been working on.

Their work focused on identifying the top five obstacles inhibiting leadership evolution. Their findings revealed that the number one obstacle inhibiting leadership is ego. This finding underscores many of the key themes in this book.

They admitted having some internal debate over the ranking order of the remaining four inhibiting obstacles but were in total agreement that ego was, by far, number one with the concept of, "operating in the ill-defined" coming in second. We'll be exploring this later in the book.

It's human nature to believe your views and opinions are right and, in turn, others' views are wrong. One clear exception is when data and indisputable facts prove otherwise. For some, ego is so powerful that even the facts won't persuade them to change their position. It's sometimes a case of "Don't try to confuse me with the facts. I know what I feel."

Whether it's politics, the disciplining of children, or events in the news, we take a position on where we stand and then firmly defend it.

The number one obstacle inhibiting leadership evolution is ego.

To have someone convince us that our thinking is wrong challenges our intelligence and value. In the workplace, this is an especially sensitive area. When a subordinate challenges the boss and the subordinate's perspective proves to be right, it could raise a question of who the leader should be.

It's obvious that no one is right all the time. It's important to show our openness and vulnerability, which leads to the question "Am I worthy to hold the seat of power?" But this can be sensitive territory on the "Ego-Richter" scale.

If one is frequently proved wrong, there may a legitimate reason to question whether that person should be leading. There is an underlying belief that saving face will save my job and even get me promoted. It logically follows then that frequently losing face may have the opposite effect.

Which is more important for one's career, seeking truth or being right? It's all about the art of balancing ideology with practicality. Since seeking truth should always be the primary objective (ideology), then it follows that you should avoid taking a firm stance on any business matter until you have solicited the broader perspective of others on your team.

I had a boss who represented the worst manifestation of this behavior. He would take a definitive position on virtually all subjective matters. It was common for him to begin a staff meeting saying, "I have this great idea I want to run by you." He believed that it was his responsibility as the leader to have a vision and provide direction for the team's success. The problem was, he felt the vision had to come from his head alone.

He believed the creation of any strategy that required vision or problem solving should come from him. He was not alone. This antiquated perspective of a leader's role remains pervasive.

Whether subconscious or otherwise, the voice in his head said: "You're the boss. You were selected for this role because you have greater wisdom, experience, and knowledge than those working for you." His thoughts were further reinforced with the refrain: "You must ensure that your team looks up to you and, at the same time, convince your bosses they made the right choice putting you in this role."

Probably everyone has had a manager who, if you could place your ear close enough you'd likely hear those words cycling on repeat in their head.

The instinct to protect our ego may be a byproduct of what we observed and experienced in our youth. Our first leaders were our parents and teachers. Children have generally been expected to be respectful and to absorb knowledge from adults. They are indoctrinated to view their parents and teachers as the experts. Parents provide knowledge, guidance, and development; and children are expected to learn. They are virtually never solicited on ways to improve the learning process. How antiquated is a system that excludes input and potential wisdom of its primary recipients. The learning process should be a two-way street. Teachers need to develop the skill to learn and appreciate the wisdom that comes from children as well.

I observed this dynamic at a higher level as a member of my local Board of Education. Hierarchy drove decision-making across the system. The focus was less on seeking the best solution and more on who had the authority to make the decision. At times, it was reminiscent of the classic militaristic command-and-control style of leadership, just missing the uniform and stripes.

This model is not dissimilar to the workplace where employees are treated as students who are expected to yield and to be deferential to the boss's invisible stripes of authority. The etymology of the word "boss" is noteworthy. It comes from the early Dutch word *bass*, meaning "overseer/master," and was the standard title of a Dutch ship's captain. It's all about power and control. And yielding to power is inseparably bonded with survival.

Survival, as a psychological driver, plays a critical role—quite literally! People need their jobs to survive. Job security motivates people to make their work status safer by pandering to the boss. Telling the boss (however diplomatically) that his or her idea is weak, laden with risk, or even flawed could be idealistically admirable but prove unwise in the arena of practicality. The risk is borne from a legitimate fear that one's compensation, upward mobility, or employment itself could be jeopardized. It is the stuff office politics is made of.

An instinctive method used to avoid the risky confrontation with an alpha is the inherent use of *MicroDeceptions*. These are subtle messages that demonstrate agreement balanced with safely testing the waters of challenge. The process of *MicroDeceptions* will be explored in Chapter 7.

It is time for an evolutionary shift. Great leaders must lay down the shields that protect their egos and aspire to a culture that places the pursuit of truth over the need to be right. After all, good ideas can come from anywhere.

THE HISTORICAL FOUNDATION OF CURRENT-DAY LEADERSHIP

It began in Rome. Although far rougher around the edges, even quite bloody and riddled with ambition, conquest, and betrayal—much of Rome's leadership roots and structure, embodied in its Senate, remain with us today.

The Roman Empire has stood as a beacon of power and effectiveness in the ways its leaders dominated the world. Although technology plays a major role in civilization's leadership and dominance today, if we were to strip away those technological advances, Rome would continue to hold its own as an indomitable force.

Rome created the original practice of cognitive diversity leadership, which continues to reverberate as a current-day aspiration. Cognitive diversity at its core became Rome's indomitable strength. While other nations' cultures remained suspicious and mistrusting of outsiders, Rome promoted a more heterogeneous culture. It was renowned for being a welcoming safe haven for outcasts and misfits. If you weren't welcomed anywhere else, you could come to Rome—bringing along with it a vast treasure trove of alternate perspectives and ideas.

This heterogeneity posed obvious risks, but the amalgamation of different ideas, from a highly disparate range of cultures, yielded countless groundbreaking engineering discoveries and architectural feats. Early Rome's culture of embracing diverse thinking and the merging of ideas enabled levels of innovation and architecture that set a new trajectory.

Many of the world's first great work projects—stadiums, palaces, roads, and aqueducts—spanned three continents and were spawned by the diverse knowledge and experiences of early Roman leaders. Although established in a bloody fratricide, the fabled story of Romulus and Remus (753 BCE) serves as a window into the power of cognitive diversity. As a misfit himself, Romulus shaped a collective body of knowledge and thought gleaned from the exceptionally diverse population that ultimately became Rome's foundational structure.

For example, in their remarkable mastery of engineering bridges, the Romans used a special concrete, *opus caementicium*—a hydraulic setting mixture blended with volcanic ash. They also engineered segmented, arch bridges. These are elegant examples of the power of heterogeneity at its best.

In its later infamy, the eponymous Rome experienced abuse and horror, and it certainly had its share of monsters and demons (few look up to Caligula or Caracalla with admiration). But notwithstanding some madness, the empire that emerged from highly diverse cultures and great minds advanced the infrastructure of the global community, and its Senate set the platform for much of the world's organized structure of leadership today.

Some of the same inhibitors to great leadership in our current workplace existed back then, as well. In early Rome, challenging your boss would likely have resulted in more discomfort than simply being handed some packing boxes and shown the door.

EMBRACE COGNITIVE DIVERSITY

Great leaders push back from the intimidating alpha model that discourages challenge. Evolved leaders sublimate their egos in the pursuit of truth. They do more than merely invite diverse opinions; they welcome and reward contributions of different perspectives and even go a step further by making the process of constructive challenge a job requirement. They operate on a platform that defines the essence of great leadership—being able to motivate and inspire others to perform to their potential.

The focus of this book is to learn from the many successes of the past while taking the helm and guiding the trajectory of leadership's future.

Your mission as the evolved leader is to be a motivational and developmental visionary. Discard the illogical natural selection process and build a team of cognitive diversity champions. We must avoid allowing past practices to influence leadership behavior in the twenty-first century. Dig down and jettison anything that obscures this mission, and raise the thinking of those around you to actively embrace a new mindset for changing our leadership paradigm.

CHAPTER 3

Culture Takes Center Stage

In past decades, an organization's culture was not a critical area of focus. Today, culture takes center stage.

In a recent analysis published in the *MIT Sloan Management Review,* researchers said record turnover is being driven by something very hard to fix—identified as toxic work culture. The researchers looked at turnover spanning a six-month period and analyzed 172 culture metrics at roughly 600 companies. They found toxic work culture to be the biggest factor that led people to quit, and exponentially more important than pay in predicting turnover.

From those reviews, the most common ways employees described toxic work culture at their company were: workers feeling disrespected, a failure to promote inclusion, abusive managers, a cutthroat environment where workers felt colleagues were actively undermining them, and a culture of unethical behavior or low integrity.[1]

Evolved leaders must master culture. The upward curve of cultural evolution is the new trajectory and will continue to rise at a breathtaking velocity of change.

If you find it difficult managing the pressures of political correctness and the vast array of evolving cultural challenges that dominate today's workplace, be assured that failing to master culture-centric leadership skills will ensure your role as one of tomorrow's dinosaurs.

You may be wondering, is this about "wokeness"? This is an important question and one that deserves to be addressed here. The term "woke" has come to imply all aspects of liberal ideology, but as with most social and political ideologies, there is a range in their spectrum of advocacy, what we call the "extremist fringes" at both ends of the spectrum.

The upward curve of cultural evolution is the new trajectory and will continue to rise at a breathtaking velocity of change.

For example, there are religious extremists who join a monastery, shave their heads, wear a Kasaya, commit to a lifetime vow of silence and celibacy, and spend all their waking moments studying their religions doctrines while literally hundreds of millions of others of the same faith practice it very differently.

For everything people associate themselves with, there are far left and far right interpretations within it. Whatever term one chooses, the application of being "Woke in the Workplace" would be best described as simply striving to promote a workplace environment and a culture that enables all employees to perform to their full potential such that their immutable profiles, beliefs, gender, race, and identities are not obstacles that impair their career opportunities and ability to perform to their potential. I would question anyone who wouldn't embrace this as an admirable and essential goal of leadership.

This is not about who should play on sports teams, or who should read stories to children in the classroom; this is solely about optimizing performance in the workplace, for everyone.

Effectively managing evolving workplace culture requires an increasingly broader and ever-changing set of skills. Doing this well demands a large allocation of your mental real estate—much of which may, and often will, fall outside your comfort zone.

CULTURE IS UBIQUITOUS

Everyone talks about culture; yet it is rarely well defined. It surrounds us in every interaction and in all that we do within a business community, but people rarely codify what it actually means. At its most fundamental level, culture can simply be described as "The way things are done here."

Companies use operating principles and value statements to give culture a shape and form in order to have its employees manifest it. Notwithstanding those efforts, it remains largely an elusive and ill-defined social and living operational presence.

Let's give this amorphous concept some teeth. Organizational or corporate culture refers to the underlying beliefs, values, and assumptions held by individuals within an organization, along with the practices and inclusive behaviors that demonstrate and support them. Culture reflects what a company considers important or unimportant, but most critically, the methods and process by which goals, projects, and day-to-day work are accomplished—and how others interact with you.

Workplace culture is an amalgamation of a company's sanctioned attitudes, experiences, beliefs, and values. It is largely driven by rules that define what you say, to whom, and when and how others respond to you, at all levels. Workplace culture extends beyond its internal orbit within a company. It influences and controls the ways employees interact with stakeholders, clients, and customers outside the organization, as well.

When asking people to describe their company's workplace culture, some of the most common descriptors we hear reach across a myriad of culture profiles. They include:

- ▶ **Nice culture.** Pleasant and affable; tone is critical.
- ▶ **Numbers-driven culture.** Hit your targets and you are widely respected.
- ▶ **Hierarchical culture.** Deferring to those who are above you.
- ▶ **Facade culture (duplicitous).** Nonconfrontational to the individual but critical behind the person's back.
- ▶ **Command and control culture.** Militaristic; take orders; do what you're told.
- ▶ **Collaborative culture.** People rarely make decisions without seeking input and agreement.
- ▶ **Smartest-person-in-the-room.** An environment of competitive egos.
- ▶ **Mean-spirited culture.** If I put others down, it elevates me.
- ▶ **Holistic culture.** Respects differences and values diversity of thought.

The list of categorizations is endless, and in some cases, it represents a unique combination of culture types. Again, it all comes down to defining "How things are done here." If you want to get along and be successful, adhere to the culture. I'll briefly describe a few cultures to illustrate some of the differences.

A major investment firm in the Midwest operates as a nice culture. This isn't to say that it sacrifices great business practices purely for being nice, but niceness is an important part of being respected and successful at this company. I recall arriving at headquarters to deliver a keynote seminar. The car service scheduled to pick me up failed to show, and after learning they would not be able to provide a backup, I was forced to call a rideshare service. Instead of arriving my usual 30 minutes prior to start time, I arrived with only 10 minutes to get to the room, set up my computer, and test the equipment.

Upon arrival, my host was waiting in the lobby. After she signed me in with security, we headed to the auditorium. She turned and mentioned that there was someone approaching she would like me to meet. "Hi George. This is Steve Young. I'm sure you've heard about the MicroInequities eLearning program we've been rolling out. Steve here is the creator and author . . . "

Shift to the thoughts inside my head: "I've only got six minutes left to get to the room and complete setting up before presenting to an audience of 300 people! I wish you had just waved and increased your gait toward the room."

A minute later, "Oh, there's Charlotte! I have to introduce you to Charlotte!

"Charlotte! Have you taken the MicroInequities eLearning course yet? This is Steve Young. He is the developer of the course and will be speaking at . . . "

Back to inside my head: "Look, I don't expect you to be rude and ignore your colleagues, but wouldn't a simple smile and a quick, 'I'll talk to you later' suffice since we only have three minutes left to get to the auditorium?" But that's not how things are done here! In this culture, it's better to be late than rude or risk appearing to be not nice to a colleague.

This was repeated not once but two more times as her colleagues approached—and yes, we arrived late to the meeting. But again, that was OK because "that's how things are done here."

The very next day, at a meeting in New York City at a major law firm, I was consulting at a strategy session for leadership development. One of the partners began describing his development plan for an employee whom he had placed on the high-potential list for succession planning. A participant lifted both hands with palms out, facing the speaker, interrupted, and said, "What are you talking about? That guy doesn't know his ass from his elbow! How the heck did you put him on the HiPo list?"

Surprisingly, no one at the meeting flinched at the harshness of his comment and tone. Even the recipient of the admonishment seemed relatively unfazed because, after all, that mean culture style was simply "the way things are done here."

It was impossible not to compare these two experiences on back-to-back days. The two business cultures couldn't have been further apart on the spectrum. I imagined extracting an employee from that friendly cultured company onto a team at the aggressive culture of the law firm, or vice versa. They would either be ostracized in one or torn apart in the other, if they failed to assimilate to the new culture.

More significantly, both represented a culture style that did not emulate what organizational culture demands for the future. Both missed the entrance ramp toward the future corporate culture highway.

The prescribed new destination is one that takes the best practices from multiple corporate cultures and forms a new evolved state. Nice cultures bring warmth, respect, and comfort but can falter in their performance efficiency. While unbuffered, mean cultures may put the dart in the performance bull's-eye but only after poking out the eyes of too many along the way.

These are only two examples of company business cultures that have not yet evolved to take center stage.

CULTURE IS RAPIDLY EVOLVING

In past decades, workplace culture sublimated individuals. People were expected to show up and do exactly what they were told—and do it well. Business was indifferent or oblivious to individuality. Bringing your personal life and how you may be different to the workplace was frowned upon and, in most cases, forbidden. In the not-so-distant past, businesses were legally allowed to terminate employees based on their sexual orientation or identity or if their personal style simply didn't fit in.

Great talent was routinely lost or stymied by these illogical and inhibiting business practices. Fortunately, those old standards have been relegated to the same archival shelf as the DVD.

We now recognize the inherent dangers of this obliviousness and indifference.

It goes without saying that demand for top talent continues to rise exponentially. It used to be that the employee needed the job and had to kowtow and conform to the command-and-control style of the business. For some time now, that model has been flipped. Businesses are aware that they must compete and create a culture that attracts, wins, and retains top talent. Paying higher salaries isn't enough.

"In a world where money is no longer the primary motivating factor for employees, focusing on employee experiences is the most promising competitive advantage that organizations can create," wrote Jacob Morgan in the *Harvard Business Review.*[2]

Many companies have rapidly evolved to place much greater focus on the importance of culture and workplace experience as integral contributing factors to sustaining their success. The shift is not an outgrowth of an act of morality or kindness, nor does it simply stem from doing good deeds. It's about strategic wisdom and recognition that acquisition and retention of top talent and resources are paramount to remaining at the tip of the spear of any market.

But that evolution has not advanced at a velocity that keeps up with the pace of changing markets. Having worked with over 400 companies across 35 countries, I can say that, clearly, many corporate cultures still lean into more traditional structures.

The evolved leader must recognize the need to reach beyond seeking talent based merely on a candidate's technical skills. Yes, the job still must get done. But, if the culture doesn't reflect their needs within the PMV structure: performance, motivation, vision, and values, you might as well have hired a temp, because the odds are they'll be gone before their first performance review.

One of the most critical skills of the evolved leader is to create a psychologically safe environment so that people are not fearful of sharing contrasting views. That old "shut up and just do your job" rubric simply doesn't fly anymore.

David Joyce, vice chairman of GE Aviation, told me, "In order to have a culture that enables people to perform well and contribute their best ideas and viewpoints, there has to be a culture in which people have the confidence to speak up."

To some, hearing this might sound platitudinous, or just common sense. Of course, it's important for people to have the confidence to speak up! This, however, is another example of the stark gap between common sense and common practice. There are very few places in which I've worked (actually only one) where before challenging the boss I didn't feel a sharp tinge of caution run down my spine.

The value of fueling a culture of psychological safety as your leadership focus shouldn't solely be relegated to large multinational companies such as GE Aviation. The application is universal. Creating a environment where people are able to productively challenge authority should be a core objective for all workplace cultures.

> There has to be a culture in which people have the confidence to speak up.
> —David Joyce, vice chairman, GE Aviation

At a vastly different type of enterprise, Cooke's Seafood Restaurant, an iconic Cape Cod family-owned business in Orleans, Massachusetts, the owner Spiro Mitrokostas shared with pride that culture is a key ingredient to their success. He believes it's the primary reason so many employees from around the world return to his seasonal business year after year.

"I tell employees on their first day, this is going to be the best place you'll ever work," Mitrokostas claimed with pride. Employees proudly confirm his claim, across a myriad of social media. He consistently hears from them that it's the workplace culture that keeps them coming back year after year.

Whether an iconic small business in Cape Cod or a multinational Fortune 500 corporation like GE Aviation, creating a culture that allows employees to speak up is a top value leadership skill that will become even more important in the future, as the business evolves along a variety of predictable and unpredictable paths.

One thing is certain. The talent selection process must account for a broader spectrum of an individual's cultural needs, dimensions, and perspectives; and organizations must provide a work environment that nourishes employees. I am not talking about the obvious offerings of telecommuting and work-life balance. The evolved leader must reach well beyond these fundamentals and incorporate a culture-centric focus that motivates and builds commitment, loyalty, and the desire to contribute toward business success.

There are numerous work environment and operational adjustments that need to be embraced and fully injected into the corporate culture for it to become the magnet that not only attracts today's talent but anticipates evolving talent requirements to match its vision of the company's future—at the same time that it inspires peak performance. This philosophy holds true for both acquiring new talent and optimizing the company's existing talent.

It is the leader's role to scour the company's landscape and zero in to identify its top talent. This is not a passive process. It involves actively sifting through and securing those "gems" that flow through your organization's work streams.

Once the individuals are identified, the leader must step beyond conventional approaches. It is no longer good enough to place their names on a high-potential list and dangle the carrot of hierarchical promotions and added work assignments. Instead, the evolved leader must use innovative techniques to cultivate the environment for talent to develop and thrive.

PROMOTIONS TO MANAGEMENT FOR A JOB WELL DONE CAN BE DANGEROUS

The archaic practice of promoting a person to manager for having done their current job well can be a tripwire that has set back the career of many a hiring manager.

The sole purpose for focusing on shaping the right culture is to attract, retain, and develop the best talent—talent that is unleashed to be creative and innovative and perform to potential. But performing well in one's current job does not necessarily correlate with being able to manage people well.

Basic sourcing and recruiting of new talent is certainly a critical component for business success. The focus of this book, however, will not be on this function. This book explores what the evolved leader must do with those resources once they have been secured to maximize team productivity and exceed the business objectives.

As we examine the concept of organizational evolution, one particular practice has remained stagnant for eons. As noted above, it is the archaic practice of promoting people to positions of management simply because they have done well in their current job. It may be intuitively obvious that this ubiquitous approach is an active landmine, but sadly, tradition has normalized it. The practice of placing people in management positions that control the destiny of others, without proven management skills, likely comes from a time when management layers were shallow, largely due to businesses being family run and nepotism ran unrestrained.

Royalty is a cornerstone example. Some of the most empty-headed people became rulers commanding entire kingdoms solely due to royal lineage. The successor was typically male (primogeniture) with unlimited power to direct his subjects to do his bidding at will. The roots of these illogical succession practices run long and deep. They extend well beyond the castles of old and into the halls of industry.

For centuries, there existed typically no more than three hierarchical levels in most businesses: a founder/owner, his son(s), and the workers. An additional supervisory layer might be added for larger businesses.

It wasn't uncommon for the eponymous business name to include the tag "& Son," making it clear who the "ruler" was and who would inherit not only the assets but the leadership control, as well. Businesses were far less complex than those of today. Poor succession choices that might prove disastrous today posed far less risk in the past.

Today, a typical multinational Fortune 500 company has seven to nine hierarchical levels from its lowest level employee to the CEO.

When assuming the role of manager, outstanding technical and proficiency skills are necessary, but they must not be the primary selection criterion for the new role. Being good at what you do should not be rewarded by making you responsible for managing people.

For example, in the world of education, someone may be a prodigy in a particular subject—but this would not make the person qualified to be the teacher.

In the iconic movie *Rain Man*, Raymond is a savant with extraordinary math skill. He is autistic but can solve virtually any equation, no matter how complex, in the blink of an eye.

In one scene, a waitress accidentally spills a box of toothpicks onto the floor. Raymond glances down and almost instantly calculates the number of toothpicks that have fallen, "246 toothpicks."

Not believing that anyone could count the random pile accurately in just seconds, his brother, Charlie, asks the waitress how many are supposed to be in the box. She reads from the box, "Total count 250." He congratulates Raymond for getting it so close, to which the waitress replies, "Sir, there are four still left here in the box."

Even with all his subject-matter skill, Raymond wouldn't be my choice to fill a math teacher opening. He would likely be a highly valued employee at NASA (as an individual contributor) but would be an abysmal project team manager.

Confusing subject-matter expertise and skills to execute one's job well with the *necessary* skills to manage and lead a team is a ubiquitous practice in the business world. It is a perilous flaw. This book challenges that status quo practice.

Different skills are required to perform at different levels of business. The five key categories are represented in the following tier structure:

1. **Leaders.** Motivate and inspire their teams to be innovative and perform to their potential. Build loyalty, commitment, and engagement. They set the culture and exemplify it in their practices.
2. **Managers.** Direct their teams, assign tasks, and set goals and measure their achievements in meeting or exceeding business objectives.
3. **Coaches.** Identify knowledge and skill shortcomings and provide development.
4. **Subject-matter experts.** Provide technical knowledge and expertise in a specific product or service area.
5. **Individual contributors.** Possess technical and execution skills.

IDENTIFYING AND VALUING LEADERSHIP POTENTIAL

Once you've jettisoned the old-world philosophy of rewarding top performance with a management carrot, you must learn how to uncover leadership skills and potential when sourcing talent. People can demonstrate leadership skills from whatever position they hold. It is not driven by title alone.

TAKE ME TO YOUR LEADER!

What does that mean? We've all seen the proverbial sci-fi movie where the arriving aliens approach the first humans they encounter, directing them to "Take me to your leader!" This demand suggests they want to talk to the person in charge.

Those aliens would be wiser to ask, "Who has the most influence here?" In truth, that is the more important question. One is always more effective dealing with those with the greatest influence, not necessarily the person with the highest-ranking authority.

If you want to get your recommendation acted upon, you'll be far more effective presenting it to the person with the greatest influence—versus the biggest title. Decisions within an organization tend to rely on input from those who are most respected. If you want to get something done or approved, pitch the person with the greatest influence.

Becoming an evolved leader requires you to build your skills from both ends of the spectrum. Become a trusted and respected influencing force to leaders within your organization. Also, when sourcing to fill a leadership position, seek out those who demonstrate leadership regardless of where they sit within the current hierarchy. Great ideas often come from unexpected sources.

UNCOVERING LEADERSHIP IN UNEXPECTED PLACES

One of the more compelling leadership stories a colleague shared was about a 45-minute ride he had taken with an Uber driver. He was heading to the airport following what he described as an all-day, mind-numbing meeting. In an effort to be conversational, the driver asked if he was heading home. He explained he'd been in town for an all-day meeting he found painfully boring and a waste of a valuable workday. He vented he vowed to avoid at all costs reconnecting with those colleagues—unless absolutely necessary.

The driver spent several minutes probing some of the specifics of the meeting and proceeded to ask several questions about his values and business objectives. She asked if he thought it would be good for the company if he were able to provide guidance to those who had upset him and discuss what caused him to feel distanced.

After a series of Socratic-style questions, she brought to focus the opportunities he had missed. She offered guidance on how he might approach those colleagues and productively discuss ways they might improve the work process that had so frustrated him.

Her questions drove him to reflect on their role in making the meeting less effective, as well as what he could have done to have driven a different outcome.

By the end of their ride, several new windows had been opened for him, sparking a genuinely new perspective on how he could play a key role in building a stronger team and how he could be viewed as an admired leader. He was pleased and grateful that the conversation had become a catalyst to improve his leadership skills—and although it had only cost giving a five-star rating and healthy tip, the value of this exchange was priceless.

This is what leadership is all about, and in his Uber driver's case, it had nothing to do with title or authority. In fact, they didn't even work for the same company! This represents one of the primary messages imbued in this book. With the right focus and skills, anyone can not only perform as an admired leader, but can do so at any level.

To identify someone's leadership potential, consider some of the following distinctions and skills for serving as either a leader or a manager, as mentioned in a *Forbes* article[3] distinguishing these roles:

- ▶ Leaders coach. Managers direct.
- ▶ Leaders create vision.; Managers create goals.
- ▶ Leaders are change agents. Managers maintain the status quo.
- ▶ Leaders take risks. Managers control risk.
- ▶ Leaders grow personally. Managers rely on existing proven skills.
- ▶ Leaders build relationships. Managers build systems and process.

We've drawn a clear distinction between the skills required for managers and the high-level skills needed to be an evolved leader. The question you must ask yourself is, are you satisfied being a manager, or are you compelled to rise to a level where you have peak influence on the motivation, inspiration, and commitment of those with whom you work? In sourcing leaders, look for these attributes as some of the benchmarks of great leadership that are often demonstrated at all levels.

EARLY EXPOSURE IS KEY TO SUCCESS

How early can the process begin? The foundation for learning leadership skills ideally begins at the earliest stages of education—even as early as pre-K and kindergarten.

Sadly, there isn't even a trace of leadership development in the curriculum of most public school systems. Although plagued with a variety of administrative challenges, many educators understand the value and importance of identifying exceptional academic talent in students early on.

Those showing great promise and potential are often plucked from the general population and placed in advanced classes or designated schools with accelerated learning curriculums to fuel and develop their talent and potential. This process helps ensure that HiPo students remain engaged and inspired to learn and don't languish in unchallenging and unsupportive environments.

The reason this insightful developmental behavior is more prevalent in our school systems and not so much in our business culture is the difference in the spectrum of talent. Within a single grade of students, some are exceptionally brilliant, occasionally even prodigies, while most others fall in the middle of the spectrum, and a few fall toward the bottom. Our education system must broaden its reach and identify and develop leadership skills, along with our STEM programs.

I recall delivering a leadership seminar to a defense contractor in Portland, Oregon. One of the employees had brought her, who expressed interest in the topic, to the session.

The student was so inspired by the experience that she took it upon herself to meet with members of the Student Leadership Council and suggested the seminar be presented at the school. Of course, there was no budget for this but knowing how valuable any form of leadership development is at an early age, I happily agreed to do it.

It's always gratifying to hear from business professionals how they plan to incorporate the concepts from our seminars into their day-to-day work process. It was even more impactful to observe teenagers resonating with the power of this message and how they could immediately apply it in the classroom, with their families, and in their daily interactions.

Vocational or leadership development exposure early in life can have a profound impact on building leadership and job skills. It provides students with an opportunity to imagine a life beyond the classroom and discover and master core leadership skills.

The plasticity of the brain is remarkable, particularly early in life when synapses are flexible, and circuits have not yet become fixed. Neuronal pathways that are consistently fired are strengthened. Those that are not used are eliminated through a process called "pruning." Neuroscientists like to say, "Cells that fire together, wire together." Opportunities to stimulate and trigger them early in life can be exceptionally advantageous and sometimes even life-changing. Some rather profound pearls of insight surfaced on the value of early exposure during two of my executive interviews for this book. One came from Mike Casey, CEO of Carter's, the largest children's clothing company (OshKosh B'gosh is its leading brand). The other came from Dara Khosrowshahi, CEO of Uber.

Casey was thrust into leadership roles at a very early age. His father instinctively knew the importance of developing his son's leadership skills early. When Mike told his dad that he had joined the tennis team, his father suggested he set his sights, additionally, on becoming team captain.

At that time, Mike had absolutely no interest in being the team's captain. He really just wanted to play tennis. However, his feelings had little influence on changing his father's position, which quickly turned into a command to just "go and do it." Reluctantly, Mike put in his bid for team captain, and to his surprise, he was given the role.

As Mike put it, "The problem was, I didn't have the foggiest idea what a team captain did and certainly didn't know how to do it." With the pressure on him to perform, he had no choice but to learn through trial and, as he put it, "lots of error." He gradually learned what being a captain was all about, and he began to do a respectable job of leading the team. He was gobsmacked when he discovered that being the team's captain was pretty cool, and after a full season under his belt, he became pretty good at it!

When he later joined the baseball team, he needed no persuasion from Dad to step up to the plate and volunteer. By his second season, he became team captain on the baseball team, as well. He had no awareness at the time that a life-changing foundational skill was being laid. By the time he was in college, being the leader had become second nature.

Casey attributes these early trial-and-error leadership experiences to why he became the youngest chief financial officer of a Fortune 500 company at just 37 years of age, CEO by age 47, and not long after, chairman of the board.

The development of any skill at an early age builds a powerful level of competence. My interview with Dara Khosrowshahi uncovered a similar story. He described how coming from a non-US business background created an early awareness of leadership and business skills and played a powerful role in his becoming the CEO at Expedia at age 36 and then CEO at Uber at age 48, where he took on one of the most visible corporate challenges in recent history.

Uber had experienced tremendous blowback from the highly public exposure surrounding workplace sexual harassment issues. The board of directors needed to be exceptionally selective in vetting and appointing the ideal leader to repair the company's damaged public image.

Khosrowshahi is the perfect example of a leader who jettisons his ego and focuses more on getting to the best solution versus being right. He is a prime example of an evolved leader whose ego doesn't interfere with the pursuit of truth. He has the unique skill of being a hands-on leader while remaining highly collaborative. He relies on the great minds and blended skills of those with whom he surrounds himself.

In our conversation about the importance of early skills development, we discussed how a great prodigy like Mozart might not have achieved such prolific musical heights had he begun playing the piano later in his youth. Remarkably, he would be the same vessel of potential but, no doubt, with a remarkably different outcome.

There are many examples of this. Simone Biles would likely not have become the greatest gymnast of all time had she waited until her teens to step onto a balance beam or leap onto parallel bars for the first time.

Early exposure could well be the magic bullet that solves global performance disparities between races and genders. Early exposure, whether in the arts, sports, sciences, or leadership, cultivates mastery of skills.

Let me highlight one other great leader whose insight reinforces this belief. Gloria Steinem, whom *National Geographic* named the world's most famous feminist, and who popularized the now ubiquitous women's title "Ms.," recognized the power of early exposure in the development of one's skills. Steinem created what became the globally recognized development program for young girls, "Take Our Daughters to Work Day"—which has now been expanded to include sons.

During my conversation with Steinem, she expressed her deep commitment and passion for enabling young girls to experience the equivalent "boy's club" ritual that had historically and automatically come with being male. The impetus to inspire girls at an early age was fueled by her acute understanding that little boys were advantaged by the cultural norms of fathers who spent "mano-a-mano" development time with their sons, whereby they unconsciously transferred knowledge and awareness of the workplace and their roles within it to their sons. Without either father or son being conscious of this developmental exchange, a natural sense of confidence, privilege, and advantage was transferred to them.

After many years of being nurtured by their fathers, when those young men entered the workplace, they experienced a natural sense of comfort, confidence, and belonging. Unfortunately, those conversations and visits to the workplace were rarely extended to the daughters. That little head start would have been enough to offset workplace gender outcomes further down the road.

Whether in the arts, sports, sciences, or leadership, early exposure cultivates mastery of skills.

The kick start the sons received was not at all the experience of young women entering the workplace. Steinem's mission was to bring balance and equity of opportunity to have young women enter the workforce on a more equal footing, with the same level of comfort and confidence as their male counterparts through this early exposure.

There is an endless list of people who have accomplished greatness when there was early exposure to concepts, skills, and opportunities. Bill Gates first began working with computers at the age of 10 and wrote his first software program at age 13.

By the time Steve Jobs was 10 years old, he was deeply involved in electronics, largely influenced by the many engineers he befriended through family in his neighborhood.

Although tennis was not a common sport in Compton, California, Richard Williams first exposed Serena and Venus to the sport at the tender ages of three and four, respectively. Their meteoric rise is legendary.

Renowned physicist and Nobel Laureate Madame Marie Curie was introduced to the process of laboratory instruction at around eight years old by her father, who brought science laboratory equipment home and instructed his children in its use.

Mozart was introduced to the piano at age three by his elder sister, Maria, and later was taught by his father, Leopold. Amadeus wrote his first composition at age five.

The correlation between early exposure and mastery of skills seems to be inextricable. Unfortunately, not everyone has the opportunity for early exposure and experience, as was clearly evidenced with those high school students in Portland, where I had been invited to present to their student council. Some students were transfixed, asked questions, and were eager to participate and learn about advanced leadership techniques, while others buried their heads in their desks and were disengaged, and a few appeared to be napping.

Many schools have learned the value of homogeneous sectioning. Not everyone agrees. Some suggest this approach runs the risk of perpetuating the lack of development for children who were not as fortunate to have had early exposure and development, and this may disproportionately affect minorities or any socially or economically marginalized group. The parents or caregivers of these students may not have had the knowledge, experience, or opportunity to provide early exposure for their children's skills development. Could this have the negative impact of leaving them behind? Let's address that head-on.

Acknowledging the social realities and causes of performance gaps we see is in no way an endorsement of perpetuating an imbalanced learning structure. The real question, whether in the classroom or the workplace, is how we can provide a customized approach to development that includes all strata of learners or employees.

Exposure, in general, expands one's universe and vision. A perfect example is the orthopedic surgeon I invited to speak to a group of 200 middle schoolers. He opened his talk with a simple question for the students: "How many of you want to be an orthopedic surgeon when you grow up?" Only one hand raised in response. Then he asked, "How many of you know what an orthopedic surgeon is?" Of the 200 children, only 1 additional hand raised.

Along the same line, his next four questions were the same, asking who would like to be a doctor, lawyer, business executive, or movie star? The vocational choices ranged from about 20 to 30 percent (yes, several of them voted twice). Certainly, no surprise to anyone.

The orthopedic surgeon then spent about 20 minutes describing the details of his profession in terms that the children could easily understand. He described himself as a carpenter and explained how he always enjoyed building things but was terrible at it. He confessed that he couldn't saw a straight line, he regularly smashed his thumb with the hammer, and he was never able to smooth a surface without ripping the sandpaper. Because he wasn't so good at it, his interest in carpentry eventually waned.

While in college at a social event, he was introduced to an orthopedic surgeon. During that encounter, he learned of the incredible similarity between orthopedic surgery and carpentry.

He became so fascinated that he made it his career choice. He brought several props for his talk and showed the children a stainless-steel knee joint, a titanium tibia, and other prosthetics. He made the bold statement that he is now a different kind of carpenter. But instead of using conventional building materials and tools, the devices he uses are made for him by factories and he has the pleasure of just putting them in the right places. "Basically," he said, "today I rebuild people. When someone has been in an accident and had part of their body broken, I am the carpenter who puts them back together again." He quipped that, "had Humpty Dumpty fallen off the wall today, he could probably put him back together again!"

He played a video clip of several before and after images of patients who had gone from broken and incapacitated to repaired and healthy as a result of his exceptional work as an orthopedist— and the best part, he said, was that he didn't have to use his poor cutting or sanding skills to make people better.

He closed his talk with the same question he had posed when he began, "Who here wants to become an orthopedic surgeon when you grow up?" This time, a sea of hands raised and waved enthusiastically. What was absolutely clear in that magic moment he had created was how much early exposure can influence vision and future opportunity.

One possible silver bullet may lie in a well-orchestrated system that introduces children to the broadest possible spectrum of pursuits. Whether in STEM, the arts, education, or business, providing a systematic solution for early exposure may bring us to a point of narrowing the divide and performance gap.

As a leader, you are not be able to turn back the clock and expose your colleagues to development they may have missed in their childhood, you can step up and take action that accelerates their skills development using the most advanced evolved leadership techniques.

EAGLES NEED TO FLY

The evolved leadership evolution has not yet occurred in the development of workplace talent. We cannot be passive. Or even merely embrace the current standards, alone. We can move to the next dimension of identifying top talent.

There are many dimensions of innovative practices that need to be embraced to become a truly future-focused evolved leader. Talent identification and development are but one facet of the broader need for an evolving perspective on culture and its impact on performance. Although there has been an upward curve of change, disappointingly, remnants of a decades-old "command-and-control" culture remain active within many organizations today.

Prestigious companies see themselves as proven, powerful monoliths of their industry. They believe their market dominance and prestige are all that is needed to attract some of the best and brightest—and they tend to be right. Job candidates who want to work within the company's prestigious headquarters often encounter a cultural hypocrisy.

Recruiters recognize the strong correlation between top talent and a profile of those who are independent self-starters and emerging visionaries. Employers exploit this profile, professing to the prospective employees how much the organization appreciates independent and innovative thinking.

Their bond is formed, and those impressive new hires are brought into the fold. Once they come on board, however, the culture message they will likely hear is, "Now that you're a part of our organization, let me tell you how things are done here." Ironically—and sadly— they hire eagles and make them fly in formation.

Many of these prestigious companies view the rapid metamorphosis of workplace culture as a mere fashionable trend—just more warm and fuzzy political correctness. For them, the focus on culture is not a front-burner issue, and some even scoff at it. Unfortunately, those who think they can sweep this evolution under the rug and continue operating in that moth-eaten status quo will have the rug snatched out from under them. It may be a hard fall and one from which it may be difficult to recover.

To put it in one company's HR vernacular, "Mr. Status Quo" is on the road to being downsized. There is a new and smarter "normal" coming to town, bringing with it an exponential upward curve in how we attract, develop, and retain talent.

They hire eagles and make them fly in formation.

We need only reflect on our recent past to gain perspective on the speed of culture change. Look at the US military. In very short order, the US Marine Corps (USMC) has gone from prohibiting LGBTQIA+ members in the military, to "Don't Ask, Don't Tell," to full-spectrum acceptance and inclusion of all identities, to women actively engaged in combat, as well as three female generals taking their seat at the USMC leadership table.

The upward curve of cultural evolution is the new normal and will continue to rise at a breathtaking velocity. The remainder of this book provides a number of ways to shape and align your skills with this new leadership trajectory and some specific techniques you can apply in the pursuit and development of top talent.

**The upward curve of cultural evolution
is the new normal and will continue to rise
at a breathtaking velocity of change.**

The bottom-line is don't allow yourself or your company to be an also-ran culture—one that plays the game but never takes center stage. Evolved leaders must stay ahead of the emerging cultural evolution and create an environment that fosters the sourcing, acquisition, and retention of top talent. Your business success depends on it.

CHAPTER 4

Connective Communication

How many times have you heard someone say, "I just don't like that guy?" When challenged to explain the reasons for the discontent, it's not unusual for the response to be, "I can't put my finger on it, but I just don't like him."

In the arena of interpersonal communication and the subtle messages we send through nuance, facial expressions, tone of voice, gestures, and even silence, I have found, in the overwhelming majority of cases, discontent is inextricably linked with disrespect. It is a conclusion that is often the result of poor connective language.

One person interprets a statement of simple disagreement as condemnation or a put-down Sometimes, casual friendly teasing is perceived as condescension. Neither of these conclusions would likely be reached if connective language were a better honed skill.

Learning and applying the skill of connective communication is a central thread for optimizing workplace collaboration and establishing a mutually supportive culture.

When water is tainted, a plant may survive but can never thrive. In our relationships, whether with spouses, partners, parents, children, friends, or workplace colleagues, a major cause of disharmony and discontent rests on "tainted," or unskilled, delivery of connective communication messages. The relationship survives, but doesn't thrive.

Connective communication is the umbrella under which *connective language* rests. It encompasses all aspects of the ways we create bonds of support. Connective language, however, is the mechanical process by which we send words and messages that cause others to feel respected, valued, and connected to a team or organizational culture.

Traditionally, when people strive to be effective communicators, their efforts focus on doing things correctly. Attention is placed on technical precision, accuracy, thoroughness, and clarity of the message. In addition to these, the evolved leader must learn to master connective communication that focuses on impact, relationship building, loyalty, and performance.

There is no correlation between being a good communicator and being effective at delivering connective language. One who is skilled at connective language causes others to feel safe and uninhibited in expressing disagreement and even dissent.

The fundamentals of basic communication are quite simple. Communication is the process of conceiving a message, then sending that packet of information to a recipient, who then interprets (or misinterprets) the message received. The recipient confirms receipt of that message with a response to the sender and, on occasion, commentary or judgment about it. This process is often mechanical accompanied with obligatory responses as required.

When connective language is injected, it conveys respect, interest, value, and engagement. This is the vital connective tissue that builds relationships and telegraphs that the sender has the recipient's best interests in mind, and vice versa.

On the spectrum of respect, basic communication tends to fall more on the cold and distant side, while connective communication tends to be warmer and more engaging. This higher end of the communication spectrum is exponentially more impactful and productive in forging workplace relationships. It is what causes those who do it well to be admired leaders.

WHAT DOES CONNECTIVE LANGUAGE LOOK LIKE?

How is connective language manifested and why is it a skill we must hone?

The fundamentals of interpersonal communication comprise distinct components; The message sends information that is either data-oriented or emotion-based.

On the data-oriented side, it is the process of sending facts, figures, or statistics. Its purpose is to provide what is or should be needed for getting something done—the *data channel.*

The emotion-based side is all about conveying feelings—the *sentiment channel.* The sentiment channel conveys, caring, and personal value—how I feel about you.

There are endless sentiment channels, each with a broad spectrum of expressions. Some basic sentiment channels are love/hate, admiration/disgust, respect/contempt, anger/happiness. One needs to become aware of the nuanced differences of messages within a given spectrum.

Not to get too deep into the weeds, but across each of the spectrums are multiple levels and obligatory or advanced delivery of the messages.

In the love/hate spectrum, sentiments can range from the amorous and passionate down to sheer abhorrence. Within each there can be either obligatory or advanced levels of connective language.

For example, you can tell someone "that" you love them, or you could use connective language to tell them "why" you love them; the latter being transcendently more meaningful and captivating.

Very simply, connective language is the skill, maybe the art, of mastering the building of threads that forge higher levels of commitment, engagement, support, and respect, at all levels.

Connective language conveys an understanding of having one's best interests in mind. This shifts the recipient's default when interpreting a message from an assumed coldness or negativity, to that of warmth and engagement.

The list of causes for our communication failures is never-ending. Sometimes, our misinterpretations are culturally sparked. They can be the result of racism, sexism, homophobia, or a plethora of other "isms" that invoke communication breakdowns and subsequent inequitable treatment of groups or individuals globally.

Poor connective language can cause the recipient to assume that someone does *not* have the other person's best interest in mind. It is not uncommon that one leaps to the negative when connective language is absent. Far too often, one's knee-jerk reaction to an unclear message will likely lead the recipient to a faulty conclusion regarding the intent of the message. A particularly revealing example that illustrates this default was a conversation I had with a colleague.

Heather had recently joined our team from another division in the company. After a few months in her new role, I casually asked, "How's it been going?"

She closed her eyes, put her head in her hands, and forlornly said, "I don't know if I can stay on this team." My saucer eyes must have said it all. She responded, "Let me explain. Frequently during our team meetings, Ellis has been winking at me when I'm presenting and even sometimes when I'm not speaking at all." I asked if she sensed any of this outside of our meetings. "Not in his words," she said, "but he still winks at me in a salacious way."

I was stunned to hear this. I knew Ellis well and couldn't imagine this being true. I pondered what I had missed. Was I just oblivious to what Heather felt was so blatant? Then it hit me. I jumped up laughing. She seemed a bit insulted that I was finding such a serious issue so funny, until I explained that Ellis has macular degeneration in his right eye. He sees things more clearly through his left eye, and frequently, in favoring that side, he closes his right eye to better focus. That motion has become a sort of tic now for him. For those of us who have worked with him for years, we have become oblivious to it.

The reason she hadn't noticed his pattern of behavior toward others was her avoidance of making eye contact, except when necessary, specifically when she was presenting or speaking. She wasn't at all convinced and gave me a look of suspicious disbelief, almost suggesting that I was coming to the defense of the male boss. But the day after our next team meeting, she strolled up, looked me in the eye, and broke into hysterical laughter, saying, "Jeez, I watched Ellis like a hawk this time, and you're right! He's not coming on to me! He's just focusing." He did the same thing to everybody when they were speaking too! My goodness, I've told a half-dozen women about what a jerk Ellis is. I've got to get back to them and fix this."

Heather's misinterpretation of the message caused a set of filters to fall into place. All subsequent interactions were filtered by what she had perceived. Of course, this is not limited to Heather's experience. For countless reasons, we hold opinions about people that are unfounded, and filters of confirmation bias kick in. Ideally, when done well, communication is a smooth two-way street where the sender of the message compiles a clear, useful packet of information and sends it to the receiver, who then interprets the message and sends a reply of receipt and understanding. When it goes poorly, that two-way street can become a one-lane highway with oncoming traffic!

Business communication is fundamentally about sending and receiving operational details that enable work to get done. It can be, therefore, cold and sterile. You get what you need to perform the tasks, but not what you need to feel valued and respected.

The evolved leader understands how essential it is to build loyalty, engagement, and motivation by ensuring that communications are regularly threaded with connected language that demonstrates respect and value of others.

Building and applying this skill can shift one's career path from flat to an upward trajectory. This is one of the great benefits of mastering the skill of connective language.

Let's look more closely at its framework.

CONNECTIVE LANGUAGE: THE SCAFFOLDING

When we look at some of the rudiments of communication protocols, they include expressions like "Please," "Thank you," "Good morning," "Good-bye" and statements like "You shouldn't have." These, of course, carry no intrinsic or substantive meaning. They are nothing more than obligatory expressions of respect and civility.

Probably two of the most common expressions designed to convey respect are "Good morning" and "How are you?" Imagine trying to explain to some extraterrestrial planet what these expressions truly mean. "Good morning" on the surface might appear to be a statement or report on the current weather condition. If that were the case, if the weather were poor, would one say, "Not-so-good morning"? In the winter, the Starman might assume that one would say, "Cold morning" and so on. Clearly, it has nothing to do with weather conditions. So what does it actually mean, and why do we say it?

In truth, its roots come from expressing a desire for the other party to have a good day. We actually use that literal expression, "Have a good day," but oddly, that is never used as a greeting. Among these morning expressions is the ever-present "How are you?" If one ever took it literally and answered with a detailed personal health report, it's unlikely the person who posed the question would ever offer that greeting again!

As a point of reference, the origins of that expression come from a time in history where it was, in fact, quite literal. More than a century ago, people's conversations were dominated by discussions of health. Medicine was not as advanced, and serious illness was far more pervasive. "How are you?" was not a throwaway line, but a genuine inquiry regarding a person's well-being.

Habit has a funny way of becoming tradition and often becomes indelibly imprinted in culture.

Whether one says, "Good morning," "Please," "Thank you," "You're welcome," or any number of other expressions that have little content value, the essence of the message still lingers because it morphed into a traditional way to convey respect.

So why is respect so important to us, anyway? It answers the age-old question—"Do I have value?"

When one receives messages that convey the opposite—being ignored, invisible, or looked down upon, then there is the perception that the person's life has no value to others. Clearly, messages that are the opposite generate self-esteem, purpose, and worthiness. This is one of the messages that humans have yearned for through time infinitum.

Allowing the tribe's leader to eat first, bowing to the throne, saluting a higher-ranking officer, and smiling and laughing at the boss's jokes are among the countless ways we traditionally convey respect. These common expressions are all expected protocols of exchange, but carry no true intrinsic value.

Habit has a funny way of becoming tradition and often becomes indelibly imprinted in culture.

This feeds into the value of focusing on our connective language. It carries a deeper and more meaningful message. Again, you can tell someone "that" you love them, but telling them "why" you do carries a far more engaging message. Sometimes, it requires just a change in tone.

Connective language can even work without changing the words at all. Even the rudimentary, "Good morning," can either be delivered with a bland, monotone expressionless manner, or with more textured voice inflection, a smile of engagement, and a sense of warmth and caring.

Although the words used in the greeting may be verbatim, our facial expression, tone of voice, and gestures make it undisputedly clear who is respected and who is not. Everyone feels the difference through these micromessages, but they are transmitted unconsciously.

Let's take a look at the three levels of mastering connective language:

- ► **Tier 1.** Indifferent and obligatory
- ► **Tier 2.** Professional acknowledgment
- ► **Tier 3.** Acceptance and appreciation

Tier 1. Connective Language: Indifferent and Obligatory

Tier 1 is the lowest level of connective language fluency. It's largely the obligatory messages of protocol. They can convey messages of indifference or even discontent. At this level, the messages can be the absence of a message all together—silence.

We communicate at a Tier 1 level in response to a topic being discussed in a meeting or other interpersonal engagement, or we might communicate influenced by the sentiment we hold toward the people with whom we are interacting. The messages sent are at best cold, distant, or neutral. At their worst, Tier 1 messages are condemning, judging, dismissive, or even sniping. These are most commonly manifested using brief, often monosyllabic expressions such as "Fine," "OK," "Sure," "Uh-huh," "Yeah." Often their subtext is tantamount to, "Let's just move on."

Micromessages often accompany what's being conveyed through facial expression, tone, and other kinds of nuances that will reinforce the indifference or obligation to respond.

Tier 1 delivery is often unconscious and falls more within the arena of obliviousness, ineptitude, or malevolence. At Tier 1, messages of disdain are generally veiled with a mask of professionalism. This tier delivers a minimally acceptable level of professional/social etiquette and nothing more. It's the stuff robocalls are made of.

Have you ever been engaged in a conversation and found yourself asking, "Are you listening to me?" What specifically was that person doing to evoke your reaction that he or she was not listening? It need not be as blatant as having one's eyes closed or nodding off while you were speaking. This connective language level inhibits the building of a supportive team, as colleagues can be left feeling invisible and disengaged.

Invisibility is a critical outcome of Tier 1 messaging. In the world of child psychology, it is not uncommon for the child who acts out to be reacting to parental messages of invisibility. The parent need not do anything brazen or aggressive to fuel the child's self-destructive behavior. Not acknowledging the child's presence or being disengaged can affect the child's sense of value. A child will seek the parent's attention even if it comes as anger, because any attention, even scolding, is better than none.

In the workplace, one of the most powerful ways to cause people to feel they do not have value is when they are made to feel invisible. When messages of invisibility are sent, people show up in body alone. Unlike the child, they don't create a disturbance, for fear of losing their income, but they do become disengaged.

Tier 2. Connective Language: Professional Acknowledgment

Tier 2 connective language is where most business interactions reside. In general, people are polite, engaging, and responsive; have good intentions; smile when appropriate; and check all the requisite boxes.

A manager, when delivering feedback, can use a range of connective language while imparting developmental information. A Tier 2 feedback message might begin with a neutral facial expression, a nonexpressive voice nuance, and the words "Let me tell you what you did wrong . . ." before delivering the performance feedback. The balance of the feedback is a perfectly polite description of how the employee's choice was substandard, accompanied by an itemized list of what to do differently next time to improve their performance, all delivered with a tone of robotic professionalism.

A standard morning greeting takes a step up from a typical Tier 1 "Good morning," to a warmer and slightly more engaging "Good morning. How's it going?" or "How was your weekend?" No doubt, that Tier 2 greeting through more engaging facial expression, tone of voice, and body language would generate a higher level of engagement.

Tier 2 speakers give conscious thought to being inclusive and respectful but fail to execute the messages well, and more importantly, consistently and equitably.

Tier 3. Connective Language: Acceptance and Appreciation

The Tier 3 objective is for the recipient to walk away knowing that the manager has their best interests in mind and genuinely wants them to succeed.

Instead of beginning feedback with Tier 2's, "Let me tell you what you did wrong," the more skilled Tier 3 manager might begin that feedback with "Let me offer some suggestions that might help next time," clearly conveying the desire for the employee to succeed and not merely to be instructed. That message would also be accompanied by facial expressions and a tone of voice of engagement that clearly convey genuine interest.

Tier 3 is not about pandering, cajoling, or placating. In fact, it can include delivering some of the toughest developmental messages. The result sets a highly demanding standard of performance, and when done well at a Tier 3 mastery level, there is no doubt the recipient knows that the sender has their best interest in mind. This skill should be applied not only for giving feedback, but when engaging in all other interactions and responses in any business setting.

You may be wondering if Tier 3 can be achieved for any relationship within or outside the workplace. The answer is, unequivocally, yes, and it should be done. At its core, it is the skill of going beyond the obligatory and rising to establish clear interest, engagement, and respect. Overriding it all is the need for these messages to be delivered with integrity.

This was a central theme from Carter's CEO, Mike Casey, who shared his thoughts about how workplace culture should operate. He said, "Integrity is more than just honesty. Integrity is transparency. It is that you are straight with people. If you have a beef with someone, you talk with them directly. If there's an opportunity that will help that person improve, you give them that feedback, directly. Tell people the things they need to know to get better at what they're doing."

Are you having honest, developmental, productive, conversations with your team? It's all about being the messenger of equitable, honest, and respectful exchanges. If connective language objectives are not part of your development goals, you may be falling short of what it genuinely takes to be an admired and respected leader.

> **Integrity is more than just honesty. Integrity is transparency. It is that you are straight with people.**
> —Mike Casey, CEO, Carter's

Are there some members on your team with whom your relationship is strained? You may think that attaining Tier 3 connective language with them is unrealistic. Let me assure you, it is not! Considering the cost versus the potential benefit, Tier 3 mastery is well worth the investment.

Connective language is the skill one must master to enable a culture of psychological safety in the workplace.

CONNECTIVE LANGUAGE: PSYCHOLOGICAL SAFETY

One of the primary benefits of mastering Tier 3 connective language is how it becomes your conduit to achieve a culture of psychological safety.

Psychological safety defines the degree to which a culture makes it safe for people to express opposing views without fear of retribution. Tier 3 mastery is the connective tissue that enables psychological safety to be achieved.

Effective delivery of Tier 3 connective language is not dependent on technical or academic language proficiency. One could have poor grammar skills or a limited vocabulary and still be a master at Tier 3 connective language. It's about demonstrating an unmistakable interest in the remarks, suggestions, and messages that others express and creating responses that acknowledge the value of what they offered in whatever form it is expressed, verbally, visually, or written. Tier 3 is not limited to how we respond alone, but how we initiate and reach out to others, as well.

Connective language is more dependent on the connotation of a message, not its denotation. Denotation is limited to the pure definition of words in a vacuum without relying on nuance. Connotation transcends the sterile definition of words and is all about the deeper essence of the message being conveyed.

The word "fine," for example, has its clear dictionary denotation definition. This is an example of another *sentiment channel*. The word "fine" can be delivered, across its full from positive to negative. It can range from a message of agreement and approval all the way down the spectrum to disagreement or even disgust. The many iterations along the spectrum are controlled by the speaker's connotation. Above all, the recipient clearly knows which message is being sent and where they stand. It is always the connotation that transcends and conveys the true understanding of what one is actually being told.

Evolved leaders avoid the slippery slope of false self-competency, believing they have performed their job well because they said the right words. Leaning on denotation in one's self-assessment of communication skills can be delusional. Sending proper obligatory tropes does not result in building team loyalty, commitment, openness, engagement, or psychological safety.

Focus instead on ensuring all your responses reach beyond the proper denotation of Tier 1, and craft not just the proper words but the connotation that instills respect and worthiness. Do this even when your opinion is in stark contrast with the other person's to help achieve a workplace culture of psychological safety.

Here's a technique that can be quite effective at generating Tier 3 connection in a group setting. When delivering your message, never speak to the group as a whole. Always pick someone among the group to visually connect with. Speak directly to that person for several sentences, as if no one else were in the room. Every few sentences, reestablish eye contact with another team member. After making a point, briefly wait, then move on. The individual team members will likely respond with a stronger sense of connection. This approach yields a palpable difference in the level of personal connection the team feels toward you. Throughout the balance of your message, continue the process, and make it your standard modus operandi for all meetings. Rest assured, there will be a visibly higher level of engagement across the team that will only continue to build over time. This tends to further fuel an environment of psychological safety.

Merely scanning a room left to right to left, tennis match style, while speaking might make you feel less anxious, but minimizes your ability to establish a meaningful connection with anyone.

You've probably been told to restate what a person has said as a way to show respect before responding. *Please don't do that!*

For example, if I were to suggest extending a project's deadline by three weeks to improve the quality of its content, and my boss parroted back, "So, Steve, if I understood you correctly, you'd like to extend the deadline by three weeks to make it better. Did I get that right?" There would be a pause as I grasped the reins tightly to keep from saying, "Do I really need to answer that? Of course, that's what I said!"

Instead, the boss could have expressed an understanding of the value of what I said by saying, "Steve, I believe you're right. Extending the deadline would likely enable us to improve the thoroughness of the final proposal and I do support delivering our best work. But failing to meet the deadline for this client could cause us to lose the deal. It could be a case of pursuing perfection at the risk of losing the project entirely."

Wherever the discussion may go next, the person offering the suggestion will likely feel their contribution was valued and respectfully considered.

Alternatively, beginning your response to the suggestion with a question before stating your position can also be an effective Tier 3 technique. In this scenario, the manager could have responded with a more Socratic question: "Steve, this client puts a lot of weight on timeliness. How would you get around the risk of potentially losing the project altogether in the pursuit of fine-tuning it?"

These examples illustrate the benefit of Tier 3 connective language. Think broadly as you consciously filter all your messages to team members, colleagues, and in your personal relationships, as well. The essence of Tier 3 mastery is your relentless focus on using tone, words, gestures, and other micromessages to convey appreciation, respect, and value, even when your viewpoint is diametrically opposed.

Connective language cultivates a psychologically safe environment where people feel comfortable to bring their full selves to work and speak freely without fear of retribution. It is inextricably linked to one's performance. This brings us to another branch of connective language—*context and permission*.

Context and Permission

When I'm speaking with someone and they appear to be disengaged or even drifting off to an alternate reality, I might playfully say, "Would you please sing the Happy Birthday song, so I know you're not having a stroke!" Although totally acceptable, and it generates a smile from a close friend or family member, such a quip would be inappropriate in today's socially sensitive workplace and would likely yield a less than positive response.

The context and nature of the relationship change everything. I have permission to say things to my wife or children that I couldn't imagine saying to a colleague. The relationship establishes a certain unique context and affords me special permission that others may not have.

Context and permission define the license one must be granted to communicate in ways that violate basic denotation protocols of what might otherwise be perceived as offensive or undercutting.

This is a particularly difficult and highly nuanced aspect of connective language. It is unavoidable for us not to feel closer to some colleagues than others. But how is that unspoken familiarity conveyed? Or, *should* it be conveyed at all?

I had a boss with whom I could openly joke and tease in the presence of others. I had unspoken license to flippantly respond to a suggestion he might offer with, "Are you out of your mind? That's nuts!" Our longstanding working relationship, trust, and closeness enabled that comfortable flow of humor. This special license to say what otherwise would be inappropriate tells both parties, as well as the observers, that our relationship is uniquely close and personal. Others, however, wouldn't even dream about making such remarks to the boss. Context and permission defined those boundaries.

In retrospect, was that behavior illustrative of an evolved leader? Today, that answer would be no. If I were put in that position again, I would not make that choice. As we look at what may have been appropriate in the past, we must question whether it should be the practice moving forward. The uniqueness of that relationship was potentially as damaging to others as to siblings of the favorite child in a family. No doubt, it made me feel special, but when one is made to feel special, it is at the risk of others feeling excluded. An evolved leader must ensure equitable treatment across a team, regardless of personal feelings.

This is not to suggest that all relationships are equal and that everyone must be treated the same. My parents had cute pet names for each other. My dad was called "Big Daddy" by my mother, and he referred to her as "Honey Buns." Imagine if our family were dining in a restaurant and after scanning the menu, my dad proclaimed, "Hey, Honey Buns, I see they have your favorite, cheesy grits and shrimp!" Assuming the waiter overheard the conversation, there might be a problem if he approached the table and addressed my mother as "Honey Buns." Let's just say, it would not go well. No one would be puzzled or wonder why it would be perfectly appropriate for him to call her "Honey Buns," yet extraordinarily inappropriate for the waiter to invoke that nickname. There was an understood context to their relationship, and my dad was granted permission and license.

To avoid potential of such inequities, most companies have policies that prohibit nepotism. Though it may be instinctive for you to allow some colleagues leeway in the ways they express familiarity or disagreement, the evolved leader must ensure consistent, equitable treatment for all.

THE POWER OF CONNECTIVE LANGUAGE

The disparity in the ways connective language is delivered may have its greatest enhancing or eroding effect when the messages are sent differently within a group setting to some versus others. We've discussed how invisibility has an eroding effect. This becomes even more destructive when the recipients of Tier 1 behavior observe the stark difference in the ways messages are sent to others.

The evolved leader not only ensures people are merely visible (Tier 2), but is keenly aware of the impact his or her messages have when done differently in the presence of others.

As an evolved leader, you need to acknowledge what a team member says, summarize your understanding of the person's key points, ask open-ended questions to allow them to elaborate, and respond with engagement and respectful, honest commentary.

Be the Tier 3 connective language leader. You'll be rewarded with engaged colleagues, a healthy workplace culture, and overall higher performance.

CHAPTER 5

Authenticity Is Not the Goal

It may be an altruistic sounding aphorism, but authenticity should not be the goal. The goal *is* the goal.

As a frequent traveler, I often find myself thrust into airport settings that make me an unintended voyeur. Waiting to board, I overheard a conversation behind me. Someone was providing counseling to a colleague who was questioning how he should behave in meetings. The advice given was a forceful "You just be yourself!" He repeated, even more emphatically, "Just be yourself!" It seemed the recipient took it in, puffed his chest, and would likely attend his next meeting with a very outspoken demonstration of his authentic self.

Do we really want to be our authentic selves in the workplace? Or should we temper this to meet our business objectives by bringing forward a persona that maximizes our ability to accomplish the objectives, as long as the behavior doesn't violate our core values?

No doubt, everyone reading this has at some point been videoed giving a presentation. For most people, the reaction while viewing the playback is fairly consistent. It begins with a silent cringe, u turn-away, a shake of the head, and with the first words being, "Oh my God, look at me! Do I really do that? I just repeated myself like four times! I just said 'like' like ten times. Why am I scrunching my eyebrows? I just snorted! I can't believe I did that!" This is typically followed by, "I don't want to be that person anymore. I need to make some changes to look more professional, more credible."

This chapter explores three interdependent aspirational pursuits of our authentic self:

- ▶ **Person versus persona.** Our core self versus the image we choose to present.
- ▶ **Ideology versus practicality.** How do we balance morality and ethics (ideology) with meeting business goals and objectives (practicality)?
- ▶ **Transactional versus emotional relationships.** To what degree should workplace relationships (transactional) rely on friendship (emotional)?

PERSON VERSUS PERSONA

Who we are at the core (person) and how we choose to present ourselves to others (persona) is a critical balancing act.

In simple terms, the "person" is how we see and react to all conditions we encounter (social, political, ethical, etc.) when we are alone and in the absence of any external influences.

The "persona" is how we choose to express, respond, or present ourselves based on the cultural settings in which we are operating at the time.

We consciously or otherwise decide which persona to present based on society's expectations for how we should interact with others. We adapt based on the desire to be positioned, socially or professionally. We alter our behavior to accomplish these objectives. The adaptation is often an internal struggle. Sometimes the person we are at the core aligns and matches the persona we've chosen to present. Other times the difference between our person and persona is striking and may even appear as stark opposites.

The decision of how far we are willing to go to shape that persona hinges entirely on the value we place on the desired outcome. The difficulty is the inner turmoil or concern of being seen as disingenuous. People don't want to think of themselves, nor would want others to see them, as fake. This inner conflict can be distilled down to managing which parts of each we let out each day, to whom, and under what conditions.

The evolved leader blends the ideology of one's true self with the well-grounded practicality that enables them to accomplish the mission.

This amalgam is an ever-adjusting blend of the person and the personas. Let's examine this as the amalgamation of three interdependent facets of self:

- ▶ **Core traits.** The indisputable and, in most cases, unchangeable aspects of self, including our sex at birth, gender, orientation, identity, race, age, and more
- ▶ **Principles.** Ethics, values, religion, and sense of right and wrong
- ▶ **Personal dogma.** Opinions, political views, preferences, general beliefs, culture, habits

Is a person being disingenuous when the behaviors they present don't line up with these values? The reality is, they virtually never do line up nor should they.

The decision of which persona to present should be reached using your skills of risk management. Risk management is a careful balancing act requiring analysis of the state in which you are operating, to minimize liability and optimize gain against the objectives you wish to achieve. It considers the benefits and downsides of presenting your core person into the mix.

In the workplace, we hear more and more encouragement to simply "Be your true self." This is a lovely and well-intended ideology. As previously discussed, running headstrong fueled by one's ideology can lead to a perilous precipice. The evolved leader blends the ideology of the true self with the well-grounded practicality that enables one to accomplish his or her mission.

Ideology is the grounded path of morality, but one should never take a walk without grasping the handrails of practicality.

In recent years, social justice advocates have fostered a new acceptance of safely presenting one's identity more publicly. We are learning to dispense with social masks that are designed to gain acceptance. This movement has encouraged more and more people to embrace the clarion call to unabashedly "Be your true self."

In some cultures, doing so can be safe. But in others . . . well, not so much. This is where the ground gets a little shaky.

How should an evolved leader's core values be demonstrated within their workplace persona? Holding fast to the full complement of your personal values and incorporating these into the way you present yourself in the workplace is always a fine art.

The burning question is how real do you want to be in the workplace? How much of that core person does one need to put forth? How does one decide what to reveal and what to conceal? What adaptations should you make to avoid appearing inauthentic?

The separation between what is authentic and what is inauthentic has many shades of gray. If I were to take the advice of just bringing my true and honest self to work, would it then be OK when a colleague I genuinely dislike sees me in the lobby at work and says, "Good morning," and I respond by rolling my eyes and walking away in silence? Why not? I'm just being my honest, authentic self.

He's a jerk! Why should the acceptance of social convention deny me the right to express my true feelings and force me into some pretentious persona? Such a position would be universally absurd.

On the other side of the spectrum, it would be equally absurd to provide someone with enthusiastic praise for substandard work simply to avoid hurting that person's feelings, instead of providing honest developmental feedback.

An interesting example of person versus persona aligned with proper risk management was Mark Zuckerberg's testimony before the US Congress on multiple occasions.

Zuckerberg is well known for his casual style of dress. If one were to create an avatar of Mark Zuckerberg, it would be him wearing that iconic gray T-shirt, jeans, and a hoodie. But each time he has testified before the US Congress, he appeared wearing a white shirt, suit, and tie.

Was Zuckerberg not being himself? Was he being fake and inauthentic? I would say no! Just imagine, if he were to ask your advice for how he should dress at his next congressional hearing, would you tell him, "Mark, you just be yourself! You stroll into that Rotunda in Washington wearing that T-shirt, jeans, and hoodie. And when they start asking you those tough questions, just flip that hoodie up over your head! Don't be a sellout; be proud of who you are!" Not even a social justice warrior would give that advice.

It might go over well in some social settings, but would not likely help Meta's standing when congressional action is being determined. He could have defiantly, and unwisely, chosen the path of ideology and shown up as he would for any other internal or client meeting. However, the evolved leader must always weigh both sides of the authenticity equation using wisdom to weigh the balance of authenticity with risk.

Again, it's the goal that's the goal, not authenticity—as long as the actions of the persona don't fall outside the realm of your core values. Always choose to accomplish the business objective. This means, no matter what the circumstances, never falsify or deny your absolute core values. But never lose sight of your true goal.

There are some who have mastered this balance of the persona. Susan Richards, a math and science educator at Pinole Valley High School in the West Contra Costa Unified School District in the San Francisco Bay Area, described her instinctive and learned skills of managing these two aspects of self.

The persona she intentionally presents to her students is markedly different from the persona she presents with her family and friends. The differences involve style, tone, tolerance, word structure, and facial expressions. Even the way she expects to be addressed is different. In the classroom the persona commands, "Ms. Richards." Among family and friends, she is, of course, "Susan."

This is not an act of pretense or being false. Ms. Richards is simply aware that in her role as educator, there are very different objectives that need to be met. There are power dynamics that should and must be acknowledged in a classroom. As with any job, using the right tools better enables you to do the job more effectively. In this case, one of the tools involves parsing her persona. Setting the protocols of classroom persona for students also builds skills around the demands of the workplace culture.

The persona we project must always convey equitability of respect. However, we reasonably choose a different style of speech when communicating with a toddler than with a teenager, differently again with a partner or spouse, and an even quantum difference with clients or business colleagues. None of these adjustments should be labeled pretentious or inauthentic behaviors, unless they violate our core values.

How to Shape Your Persona

In light of the high sensitivity that people sometimes have managing the potential dissonance between person and persona, let's spend a bit more time bringing the management of dissonance to life for actionable application.

The decision to forge a persona should not emanate from your gut. Your risk management process in shaping it for the workplace should carefully consider personalities, hierarchy, industry, and other factors that define the culture in which you are operating. Some might see this as playing games, succumbing to office politics, or surrendering to assimilation. In this case, assimilation should not be viewed through a pejorative lens.

> Evolved leaders must have the agility to assess
> each audience or individual with whom
> they interact and adapt their persona,
> while never being untrue to their own core values.

When doing business in France, I adapt. I use my best French when speaking with clients. In Madrid, it's my best Castilian Spanish, and in writing, the culture prefers opening remarks that would sound over the top or flowery to the ears of an English speaker but considered quite normal in that setting in Madrid. When presenting to partners at Wall Street law firms, I dress a bit more formally, but I choose the opposite sartorial style with my Silicon Valley clients. Demeanor adjusts, as well. When speaking to members of the Joint Chiefs of Staff, my demeanor is more formal, whereas the same presentation to a social media company is far more casual. It's a choice reflecting business wisdom and good risk management.

These behavioral shifts are done in a semiconscious way. Instinct tends to kick in when we speak with a senior executive who controls our destiny in the ways we maintain eye contact, smile, or respond politely to the executive's remarks. When speaking with a colleague, all of that is likely to shift to a more affable persona.

It seems obvious that one would make these adjustments to be effective with clients in the workplace. The evolved leader develops the skill to understand the broader, underlying logic for making many other adjustments at a variety of persona levels—sometimes known as "code switching."

CODE SWITCHING

It's not about being a fake or being pretentious. It's about identifying the language, style, and culture that define the environment in which you wish to succeed.

Oftentimes, conversational "code switching" carries a pejorative inference. The word "switching" conjures an image of turning a switch on or off. Flipping switches certainly sounds manipulative or pretentious. Who could ever be proud of being pretentious or manipulative? This is one of the universal dangers of labeling. If the practice were, instead, called "cultural adaptability," it would likely be viewed as an admired skill.

After presenting a seminar in Chicago, a senior manager approached me with an intriguing smile. He revealed that adjustments in his persona change the actual language he chooses to use based on the culture in which he is operating. He said he was from a small rural town in Texas where the language style is very different. When speaking to clients and colleagues in the Chicago workplace, his speech patterns and vocabulary are dramatically different from how he speaks in Texas. He mentioned that just before our seminar began, a team member asked about the agenda for an upcoming meeting. He responded with, "I'm in the process of preparing it now." Immediately after, he received a call from his dad, but told him he wasn't able to talk right now because he was "fixin' to do up an agenda."

Never could he fathom using the words "fixin' to" or "do up" in the workplace. That persona would damage his image as a senior corporate leader. Conversely, if he were back home visiting family and used the expression, "I'm in the process of preparing," he would undoubtedly be considered a pretentious, pompous ass.

This is not merely opinion. He went on to share how he had slipped up at home once using his professional language and was summarily ridiculed for being a sellout. He closed the conversation with yet another example, saying, "They learned me something!"

For some, this becomes an issue of morality. They question whether it's more important to be true to one's core self or succumb to an almost theater-like persona in order to have the greatest impact. Evolved leaders must have the agility to assess each audience or individual with whom they interact and adapt their persona, while never being untrue to their own core values.

IT'S A BALANCING ACT

In Chapter 1, we introduced the concept of ideology versus practicality. Now, let's a closer look at how we place them on the fulcrum. How do we balance our aspirations for morality and ethics with our business goals and objectives?

All of us have an instinctive sense of right and wrong within our personal and professional lives. The pursuit of ideology, whether teleological or deontological, should reign supreme as the filter we apply for ethical decision-making. The workplace doesn't always allow us to play by those grand precepts. It never lets us lose sight of the reason the business exists—being profitable.

But as the saying goes, "Good guys finish last." Many of the world's most admired social-change ideological icons and Nobel Laureates for peace spent many a night, sometimes years, in prison, or sadly worse. In society, such idealism is often viewed with admiration and respect. In the workplace, however, it can take you out of the picture! It's obvious we must maintain a balance. But which tilts your scale more heavily? Being the good guy or winning?

Be true to your ideology while keeping a careful and skilled eye on practicality, so you can live to play another day.

In the United States there is a clear demarcation between church and state. Government policies and laws must exclude personal and emotional commitment to religion. For some, the church represents things that are all good and righteous—*ideology*. Whereas government represents an entity that enables a community to operate effectively—*practicality*.

A judge who may hold a personal ideology of tattoos being a desecration of the body must not allow that personal bias to influence his or her jurisprudence responsibilities when rendering a sentence. These conflicting elements often insinuate themselves into *our* judgments, as well. Our personal views must remain separate from our professional decisions and actions.

In choosing the right persona, it is paramount that you never deny your core personal values. A Black person should never have to pretend to be White, a gay man should never carry the pretense of having a girlfriend, nor should a woman feel compelled to dress like a man.

People should not have to mask their identity, religious beliefs, morals, or ethics. On the other hand, adopting a more aggressive communication style, which may be vastly different from your natural style, in a business culture where that is rewarded should be your aim.

All that we've discussed about the balancing of ideology versus practicality, person versus persona, and the business goal as the driving objective for framing your actions, paradoxically, does not hold true for our personal relationships. In the workplace we have colleagues and coworkers—while personal relationships are friends, acquaintances, and loved ones.

TRANSACTIONAL VERSUS EMOTIONAL RELATIONSHIPS

All workplace relationships are transactional in their basic structure and function. Personal relationships, such as family and friends, are emotion-based relationships.

When people hear the term "transactional," it may conjure up images of cold indifference or detachment. That is not the case here. In this context, "transactional" specifically refers to the primary purpose or nature of the relationship. People are engaged in a transactional relationship primarily for the purpose of getting work done. Another way to view it—transactional relationships are rooted in the brain, while emotional relationships are rooted in the heart—they are primarily about feelings, not performance.

Transactional relationships have, as their targets, getting the job done well, driving performance, and achieving a set of goals, all of which are often measured by revenue, growth, and profitability.

Emotional relationships share none of those attributes. They do not revolve around tasks, performance objectives, financial targets, or profitability. They rest solely on the metaphorical heart and are entirely about feelings, acceptance, comfort, and sometimes love.

Although both categories have some elements of the two criteria, it is purely a matter of balance—or in this case, designated imbalance.

Personal relationships are low on the transactional scale but high in emotion and authenticity. These emotions represent the scaffolding of what binds the relationship. The transactional component represents a small trace of what defines that connection. My children could be outstanding in their transactional performance with me. They might visit me regularly, help with all the tasks at hand, be there to answer questions I might have, perform marvelously in school, and check everything off the list of what a great child should do. In other words, their transactional ratings might be quite high.

On the other hand, suppose I overheard one of them in conversation with a friend saying, "My dad is such a jerk. The only reason I do all those nice things is because I don't want to get left out of the will." That would be devastating. Although the transactional elements would remain intact, it would lay to dust the scaffolding of our personal relationship.

The most important part of that relationship is our emotional connection. Warmth and sentiment are essential elements of a personal relationships. Skills and abilities to perform tasks only remotely play into the value of those relationships.

In the workplace, the balance is reversed. Unfortunately, because we spend so much time with colleagues in the workplace, people often blur the lines of transaction and emotion, creating an imbalance that puts more weight on the emotional side of the relationship scale.

It's fascinating how we tend to maintain this separation in other professional relationships. I've had the same doctor for many years. Our relationship is primarily transactional. We don't come together because we are friends. We only meet when there is a medical reason. Of course, there is an element of warmth and pleasantness, but it is predominantly a transactional relationship. I am there for him to fix me. I don't particularly care if he likes me or whether he's being authentic to his true self. I only care that Dr. Gorman is current on medical procedures and is great at what he does as a medical professional. It would be comical for me to come home, after a visit to his office, and tell my wife I had a concern that Dr. Gorman didn't seem to bring his true self to work.

The same is true for my relationships with our accountant, lawyer, plumber, and electrician. There is certainly an element of friendliness and warmth, but if they were to screw up any of the requisite transactional tasks, they'll get one warning, and then I'd move on to a new service provider.

That would not be the case if my daughter forgot to pick up the dry cleaning or forgot to walk the dog. I might be a bit perturbed, but it would in no way damage the foundation of the relationship, which is rooted in our emotional connection.

A dear family member recently underwent seven months of cancer care. The oncologist was cold, unfriendly, and socially awkward, but she is rated among the top three best oncologists in the state. Rest assured, should I ever need an oncologist, she will be the first I reach out to.

In raw terms, I don't give a damn what any of those providers do outside of our transactional interactions. I only care about their skills and expertise in accomplishing the objectives for which they've been hired.

Admittedly, I get some pushback from those who feel the workplace should include warmth, friendship, and personal engagement. Some have said these are among the most important attractions in choosing where to work. Those sentiments are certainly understandable, but fundamentally flawed. If you come to work primarily for the emotional connection with colleagues, then your eye is not on the prize. Emotional relationships are prone to conflicts, causing hurt, upset, distance, and anger. Should this occur and the relationship goes south, then so too does your work commitment and performance.

The ability to provide honest developmental feedback can become encumbered when emotions define a significant part of the relationship's parameters. This is the central reason that most large companies have formal HR policies strictly forbidding nepotism. Schools prohibit a teacher from having his or her child as a student. Conflicts of interest cloud everything about the ways you are perceived by others and your ability to assess, rate, and discipline those with whom you have a significant and close personal relationship.

This is not to say that workplace relationships should be devoid of emotional and personal connection. It's part of human nature to connect with those with whom we spend a great amount of time. It's good to be friendly in the workplace, but it's the balance that we must carefully manage.

Oil and Water

One example that illustrates the daunting task of balancing ideology with practicality and person versus persona in the workplace was demonstrated by John Farrell, former executive vice president of human resources for the largest commercial bank in the United States, JPMorgan Chase Bank.

Farrell was a very devout Catholic. In those days, the Catholic Church was not yet at a level of acceptance of the LGBTQIA+ community. But the bank for which Farrell worked embraced aggressive policies and practices in support of that community, in stark contrast to Farrell's personal beliefs.

On the surface, this presented what would appear to be an authenticity conflict for him as the bank's senior HR executive. How could a devout Catholic like him be a champion for the LGBTQIA+ community at JPMorgan Chase? No matter how much you shake it, like oil and water, the disparate views and opinions could never blend.

Farrell had a deep appreciation and understanding of the importance of separating his personal self from his business persona as necessary in supporting his executive leadership role and success.

As a close confidant, I had shared with him the rumblings about employee perceptions of a clear conflict of interest. How could the man who had a close personal relationship with His Eminence, the Archbishop of New York, be a credible executive leader responsible for the practices and policies supporting the LGBTQIA+ community at Chase Bank? After all, his personal morals and the bank's policies were a virtual textbook example of immiscible values. John was determined to shed and even shred that shroud of doubt.

He decided that he would become the executive sponsor for the LGBTQIA+ employee resource group (ERG). I had the dubious pleasure of delivering this news to that ERG's leadership.

Needless to say, this was not met with a warm, enthusiastic embrace from its members. To be perfectly clear, the exact response from their chairperson was, "What the f***?!! You've got to be kidding!" The chairperson was dumbfounded and said, "Steve, that's probably the most preposterous thing I've ever heard." The tirade continued, "Everyone in this company knows Farrell's religious commitment and opposition to our lifestyle. We'd be far better off not having an executive sponsor at all."

It was a difficult discussion, but I explained it wasn't a choice. If the group wanted to continue to be a recognized entity by the bank and receive funding and use of company facilities and resources, it would need to accept John as its executive sponsor.

There was one concession I was able to offer as solace. If after 60 days the group felt uncomfortable with him in that role, John would offer to gladly step aside and pass the mantle to another executive.

Within the very first week, he scheduled two meetings with the entire group in which he helped the members formulate a highly effective mission statement, established a developmental template for all the LGBTQIA+ members, took on direct mentorship responsibility for six members of the group, and offered a plethora of outside support and resources for building the group's business success.

Within the first few weeks, each of the selected six protégés had attended several executive meetings where he sponsored them and established networking connections across several business units. During three private dinner meetings, he sponsored and outlined his most effective techniques for navigating obstacles frequently encountered in the workplace. For each of these obstacles, he had them practice role playing, giving detailed feedback and guidance.

After having gotten to know their interests and business aspirations, he sourced job opportunities and secured impressive promotions for two of the LGBTQIA+ members, one of whom received a job offer for a quantum promotion. In their first meeting, John had a photograph taken of the group with him, which he framed and proudly displayed in his office.

The career development, feedback, counseling, recognition, networking, and general support the group members received far exceeded their previous experiences with executive sponsors, by orders of magnitude.

At the end of the 60 days, I reached out to the group's leadership team to pulse the state of affairs. The response was no surprise. The members enthusiastically declared John Farrell to be the best executive sponsor they had ever had or could imagine having.

I met with Farrell the next day to share the ERG's feedback. His response set the framework for what became the genesis of my understanding of the critical distinction between person and persona.

I remember his words verbatim still today: "People should never judge one's ability to do a job well based on their personal sentiments. They should be judged only on their knowledge, skills, and commitment to excellence. When I step through the door of this bank each day, I am the executive vice president of human resources for JP Morgan Chase. My personal feelings should have no bearing on determining my ability to execute the required tasks of this job."

He explained that there are many areas where his personal views conflicted with the bank's policies or procedures. He personally disagreed with some of the financial products and strategies, but once policy becomes a part of the bank's business process, it was his responsibility to support and enforce those decisions to the best of his ability.

"Those who know me understand I accept nothing less than excellence from others and certainly of myself, and that philosophy holds true across all areas," he explained. He was well aware that the bank was committed to ensuring all employees were entitled to and enabled to perform to their fullest potential and that the bank's culture was to give special attention to those groups that had been disenfranchised to bring them to a level of equity.

I often share John's vision publicly at conferences and with corporate leaders. Sometimes I do get pushback. I remember being asked, "Are you telling me that if you learned one of your direct reports was a member of the KKK, you wouldn't act differently toward that person because of your commitment to do your job properly?"

This would be an extreme test of my resolve, but the concept remains sound enough to apply even to that scenario. When presented with this personal paradox, my response is an unwavering "Yes, I would not act differently."

If that employee exhibited the same behaviors toward me, as with others on the team, and demonstrated respect, openness, and engagement, my leadership actions would be delivered equitably, as long as those social political messages and behaviors were kept out of the workplace.

The evolved leader must be skilled at not allowing emotions and the heart to obscure the messages of equity, logic, and reason.

CORE MESSAGE

Let's not live by the popular platitude that we should all just be ourselves in the workplace. Be the persona that accomplishes the objective without violating your values. It's fine for a workplace culture to be friendly, warm, and engaging, but ensure that these elements are not the dominant factors motivating your behavior.

Your primary reason to be in the workplace is to provide intellect, insight, creativity, and innovation and accomplish complex business goals and objectives.

Let your heart dominate actions at home. Let your brain lead in the workplace.

CHAPTER 6

Is Humility Overrated?

Is humility overrated? As controversial as that may sound, the answer is yes!

When examined in the context of an evolved leader, the long-standing halo that shines over humility, praising those who are humble, can be hazardous. The danger of putting too much emphasis on humility is that it inadvertently stymies many a career. It can become an unproductive virtue signaling that people admire your humility at the expense of career advancement.

No matter how talented or skilled you are, you ultimately will be that tree in the forest that falls that no one hears—if you don't make others aware of your strengths, skills, and the value you bring to the business. We call this *productive advocacy*.

The effort to appear humble in the eyes of your colleagues can often be a hazardous pond of quicksand disguised as a comforting pool of admiration. One unwittingly steps in and gets slowly pulled down, and once in deep enough, there's little chance of self-extraction.

Imagine the employer as the buyer and the employee as a commodity. The buyer's objective is to seek products that enable the business to be profitable and successful.

No matter how great the product, shoppers are less likely to buy what is difficult to see.

In all retail, certain products sell better than others. When a business recognizes the value that a particular product brings to its success, it invests heavily to ensure its sustainability. With prioritized positioning, whether through search engine optimization (SEO) or through IRL (in real life) visibility and advertising, businesses strive to create the best possible environment for those commodities that generate the greatest revenue and most favorable company image.

Other products may have value, but priority is always granted to the top seller. The key question is, how does something, or in this case, *someone*, get pushed up to maximum internal SEO prioritization and visibility?

No matter how great the product, shoppers are less likely to buy what is difficult to see. The probability of success hinges greatly on gaining access to that prioritized positioning for visibility.

In business, this plays a major role in determining your career trajectory. The challenge is in being able to artfully convey the product's qualities (your attributes) while balancing the hazards of appearing to oversell.

Buyers—in this case, bosses—are drawn to "buy" using three key selection criteria: awareness of the product, its quality, and its value. No matter how good a product may be, these three selection criteria always prevail.

The buyer must be aware that you exist, understand your specific skills and potential, and recognize your applicable value to the organization's success. This may seem self-evident, but there is often an enormous delta between the proverbial common sense and common practice. Logic and execution often remain distant partners. Things that are rational are often left in the abyss of logic and never make it through the door of action.

Overweight people are generally aware that diet and exercise will result in a happier, healthier lifestyle. Yet despite knowing this, 40 percent of Americans (ages 20–39) and 45 percent (ages 40–59) are overweight and fail to change their behavior.[1]

People are even more out of shape when it comes to managing their *"self-promotion"* health.

SELF-PROMOTION VERSUS BRAGGING

It's essential to draw a distinction here between bragging and well-executed productive advocacy. People often confuse the tastelessness of bragging with the valuable benefits of self-promotion. Too often, these get lumped together in one big pot of déclassé behavior.

Bragging is offensive because it is rooted in arrogance and the putting down of others. It focuses on turning off the light that shines on others, in order to shine the light on you. It is throwing a competitive gauntlet to make others lose so you can win.

On the other hand, self-promotion or productive advocacy focuses on making your qualities and skills known to those who should have an interest or need to know. Self-promotion is not about maligning or putting others down. It's about aligning you with the selection process of career growth in your company, profession, and industry.

Political campaigns are perfect examples of how these two styles of communication diverge. Although there is sometimes a gray line separating them, campaigns use both attack ads and promotion ads.

Some attack ads are so extreme that they reveal nothing at all about the candidate's value or plan of action. They only address the negatives of their opponent. In contrast, promotion ads focus primarily on the value and attributes of the candidate, not on the opponent.

There is a fine line between bragging and self-promotion that permeates many of our social interactions, as well. One of the most common complaints about social media is the perception that it has become a platform for flaunting oneself. The subtext of many social media postings might as well be, "Look at me, everybody! Aren't I wonderful?! Isn't my life grand?! I'm way more interesting and more successful than you, and here are the pictures to prove it!"

I often hear this lament from colleagues and friends: "I can't stand going on social media and reading posts from people who spend their time boasting about themselves." There is widespread contempt for this telegraphing behavior that drips with braggadociousness.

Conversely, we seem to admire and value those who appear humble and even a bit self-deprecating. We've all heard it a thousand times, when someone says: "I just adore her. She's so humble, you'd never know she . . . ," and then proceeds to promote all the accomplishments that person has not communicated about herself.

While I was taking a casual stroll in the neighborhood with some friends, they pointed out the home of a world-renowned musician. They made it a point to mention how modest his house was compared with many of the surrounding homes. Their tone seemed to suggest admiration and great respect for his choice to live in a home so far below his means and stature. This would be admirable only if a modest home was all he desired. But why should this be inherently good? But why shouldn't that be considered merely a personal choice versus a badge of admiration?

The fact is, neither of the bookended behaviors—self-deprecation or bodacious bragging—is productive or beneficial. Neither behavior supports accomplishing our recommended objective, which is building awareness of the product (you), its quality (how good you are), and its value (what you bring to the business). Well-executed self-promotion does exactly that.

So what's really behind this universal mission to be humble? Why do so many people avoid remarks that even hint of self-promotion?

The epicenter of our pursuit of humility is rooted in the frailty of the human psyche, which is constructed for our survival. We are wired to discern threats or challenges to our position in the pecking order.

Bragging can be interpreted as a primal signal of people pushing themselves above while pushing you and others down by default. Our tribal instincts alert us that a gauntlet has been thrown down and a defensive position needs to be struck, posturing ourselves for battle.

While listening to someone brag, we may subconsciously replace the person's actual spoken words with "I am better than you," or "I deserve more than you," or even worse, "I will take the focus away and make you invisible."

Failing to effectively self-promote pushes us even deeper into that quicksand of lost opportunity.

We fear these messages will cause others to look down on us for seeming arrogant or full of ourselves. Bragging often does carry this offensive undertone. Self-promotion, on the other hand, is merely providing logical information that ought to be a part of any succession planning process or project assignment.

The difficulty is the two are often confused. And there are many examples where social convention interferes with what would otherwise be beneficial.

Some men are reluctant to shake hands with a female colleague fearing it may be misinterpreted as a nefarious advance—so why take the risk? Similarly, some people fear that talking about themselves may be taken the wrong way—so why take the risk?

Failing to effectively self-promote pushes us even deeper into that quicksand of lost opportunity.

THE TRAJECTORY TOWARD SUCCESS

Humility focuses on not wanting to be seen as an adversary, and we go to great lengths to avoid anyone misconstruing our remarks as initiating the competitive battle. This is done so much, that self-deprecation is often valued over reasonable and logical self-promotion.

"Wow, your outfit looks great!" often receives the humble response, "What, this old thing?" (signaling that the person is not a threat), when instead a simple, "Thanks, this is one of my favorites," would be an appropriate (and probably more honest) response conveying confidence and appreciation.

Self-promotion and confidence are key attributes of "getting seen" and being recognized as a valuable business commodity. After all, the world is a competitive playing field. Self-promotion proactively puts you on the radar for advancement and opportunity. Being meek, mild, or soft more likely will get you nothing but social compliments about your being so humble.

One illustration of this came early in my career with the executive vice president of a major financial institution. As the head of human resources, he had more than 1,500 employees in his sphere of control. He had taken an early liking to me and frequently imparted developmental advice that still influences me to this day.

His quarterly meetings were open to all employees within his domain globally. Those in the metropolitan New York City area attended in person, while others attended remotely.

Just prior to the start of one of these meetings, he and I were discussing a current project. He looked at the time and realized he had to get on stage to begin the meeting. As we parted, he noticed I had begun walking down the aisle toward the back of the auditorium. I heard him call out my name. I turned and headed back, assuming he had another question about the project. Instead, he simply asked, "Where are you going?"

Puzzled, I explained that I was heading to take a seat. He followed up with, "Where?"

I replied, "Somewhere in the middle, I guess."

He might have continued his Socratic style of inquiry had there been more time but instead got directly to the point, "Steve, look around this room. Everyone seated in the rear third of the room is likely in the lower ranks of the organization. It has little to do with their skill or knowledge and everything to do with hierarchy. Somehow, they don't feel worthy of sitting with the SVPs, managing directors, and other senior executives."

His next remarks crystalized the underpinnings of the career advancement process: "The chances of getting on the high-potential list diminish with each row further back one sits—the consequence being you become less likely to be considered when an opportunity opens up."

I took it all in. I thought I was showing insight when I responded, "Great, that will give me an opportunity to get to know them better."

To which he replied, "Sure, but that's only part of it. It's far more important for them to get to know you! After all, you don't make the leadership hiring decisions; they do. Take a seat up front!"

It was one of the best pieces of career advice I have received—and a good example of how humility is truly overrated. My social instinct was to be humble and not push myself into the forefront. I no longer chose to sheepishly slip into the invisibility abyss of the room. I no longer felt it was being pushy to place myself front and center. As a result, over time, I got to know the two dozen most senior ranking executives in the division, as he had so insightfully advised, and more importantly, they got to know me.

In building those relationships, I didn't brag or toot my horn. Had I done that, the doors would have closed. In a nonboastful but effective, self-promotional way, I simply made them aware of my interests, skills, accomplishments, and creative ideas. Those relationships accelerated my rise through the organization and enabled me to develop a close rapport with the CEO and senior executives of the company.

Throughout the process, the art of executing this well is as important as the message itself. Bursting in and talking about how great you are and touting all your accomplishments will have many hands pushing you gleefully in the direction of the quicksand.

One way to artfully manage this delicate balance is to begin with questions soliciting advice and perspective. For example, when sitting in the front rows with those senior executives, after introducing myself and exchanging pleasantries, I would soon lead the discussion toward asking, "What is it that makes your organization successful?" Predictably, their answer would include an acknowledgment of the skills and abilities of their people.

These discussions revealed the skills that each executive valued. I listened, absorbed it, and very intentionally refrained from sharing any of my skills that aligned with those they valued—at least not in that moment.

In subsequent meetings I might share an article I had seen that dovetailed with their interests or needs. Only when the time seemed right did I self-promote and seize the opportunity to share any personal accomplishments for which I was proud, very consciously including words that aligned directly with their needs.

SHAPING AND CONVEYING VALUE

Let's reflect on the three key selection criteria: awareness of the product, its quality, and its value. All three were carefully integrated in my discussion with those leaders:

▶ I stayed on their radar and made them aware of who I was by sending them value-added articles or providing them information of interest that might be helpful to them.

- ▶ I outlined my qualities and skills that aligned with the ones they most highly valued.
- ▶ I established my value by discussing ideas and concepts that could support their business.

When these are conveyed, particularly as they align with business interests, opportunities are created.

You may win the congeniality trophy, but will not likely walk away with the crown if you are not on the radar of those who can champion your advancement.

When you are classically humble and self-deprecating, people will speak of you with words of warmth and congeniality, "He's such a humble guy," but what ends up being conspicuously absent is, "Let me tell you how great he is."

You may win the congeniality trophy, but you will not likely walk away with the crown if you are not on the radar of those who can champion your advancement.

Make It Personal

There is a startling difference and contradiction in the ways we convey self-promotion in our personal lives. In personal relationships where hierarchy and competition are not in play, people tend to be more comfortable with openly sharing their accomplishments. When spouses or partners come together at the end of the day, it is not unusual for them to share their incredible accomplishments without reservation. Not only is this unbuffered sharing normal, it is expected and would be oddly dysfunctional for it not to happen.

If a child were to come home after school bursting with pride at sharing a high grade achieved on an exam and that score also happened to be the best in the class, neither parent would look at the other and say, "What a braggart she is!"

Imagine the awkwardness if the child were to conform to social convention that dictates that she shouldn't brag and instead humbly declined to share the accomplishment. As a parent, I would be stunned and disappointed if the first time I discovered this was at a future parent-teacher meeting.

It seems a remarkable disparity. Why is it perfectly OK to share our accomplishments with those we love and trust, and yet sharing that pride with colleagues, neighbors, or friends makes us seem arrogant and full of ourselves?

How is this disparity in behavior logical? Not only is it a strange contradiction, but it is ultimately self-destructive.

In every venue outside the family structure, we are encouraged to be reticent and not laud our skills and accomplishments with one exception—the job interview.

Whether the interview is conducted face-to-face or virtually, the hiring manager is focused on one objective—finding the best and most qualified person for the job.

Second only to the family, the job interview is the only other setting where near unfettered sharing of one's skills and accomplishments is expected and appreciated.

The important question here is, why shouldn't we be aware of the accomplishments, capabilities, and skills of those with whom we work in all business settings?

So How Can We Fix It?

A cornerstone of the human condition is the need to have value. We must learn to artfully manage the representation of our value and skills without appearing to be rattling our swords of competition.

It is a daunting balancing act. It begins with learning the micromessages that diffuse bragging as a perceived act of competitive challenge. Instead, send messages that feature your value, skills, and competencies and show how they relate to the business requirements.

Some corporate environments have formalized the process using talent inventories. This requires all team members to list and describe the skills they bring to the organization. These inventories are often broken into two categories: the skills that are needed or applicable to the current job and the broader skills that are not currently required but may provide value in the future, or in other areas of the business.

Each category includes a section for specific accomplishments, awards, affiliations, licenses, or other credentials. It is a logical and productive process that enables the sharing of one's accomplishments and skills, unencumbered by the fear of being misperceived. It's your chance to have your "humble pie" and eat it too!

BECOMING THE EVOLVED LEADER— MASTERING PRODUCTIVE ADVOCACY

We have established that informing others of our skills, abilities, accomplishments, value, and aspirations is a wise and logical business objective.

Unlike childhood experiences, in the workplace, not everyone gets a gold medal for participation. In business, there are clear winners and losers. Players are picked for a team because either they have demonstrated success, or they have established a belief in others of their skills and high potential.

For those rooted in the belief that promoting oneself may still feel awkward, view it through the filter of "Productive Advocacy."

Self-promotion, or productive advocacy, is the process of connecting your skills and value to the identified needs of the business.

Productive advocacy is about creating a mutually beneficial exchange of information where you obtain a broader and deeper understanding of what is valued in order for the business to understand your skills that align.

Business doesn't operate on the ethereal notion that good things will happen if you passively wait. People get jobs or get promoted based on their recognized value.

"Karma" and "career" should never be used in the same sentence. Evolved leadership requires visibility and action.

Productive advocacy is the process of connecting your skills and value to the identified needs of the business.

About a year ago, I was sharing some of these concepts and skills with my nephew Brian. He was initially resistant to talk about his skills and accomplishments for fear of being perceived as too ambitious and self-aggrandizing. Up until then he had always defaulted to understatement and reticence. When he fully grasped the important distinction between self-aggrandizement and productive advocacy, a lightbulb turned on. He shifted gears.

I later received a jubilant call from him reporting that he had just received a quantum-level promotion along with a nearly 30 percent salary increase. He was convinced that this was all primarily attributable to his active use of productive advocacy.

"Karma" and "Career" should never be used in the same sentence.

Earlier I mentioned the advice I received about sitting in the front row among those in power. This was an example of the first stage of productive advocacy. Let's take a closer look at how to mine this opportunity.

Three Steps to Productive Advocacy

Each of the following suggested actions supports productive advocacy. As an evolved leader, you should not only apply these techniques for your own benefit but use them to provide guidance and development for those who report to you.

1. Start with Inquiry

Although the main goal of productive advocacy is self-promotion, you will never succeed if you begin by talking about yourself.

As mentioned earlier, people are always more receptive to questions about themselves. This is the best way to begin and open the exchange of information.

People engage more willingly when the focus is on them. This doesn't mean we should lose track of the primary mission of productive advocacy. But how do we get around this challenge of extolling our value without being seen as egotistical?

Ask questions about others—ask what their interests are, what they value, and what skills may be needed that are currently not in the pool of the team's resources. For example:

▶ "Tell me about your department."
▶ "What are the top skills required for people to succeed in your area?"
▶ "Are technical skills or analytical skills more valuable for your group?"
▶ "How is the business culture of your group similar to or different from other business areas?"

These are merely springboards for discussion that can evolve organically. Be certain to keep the discussion centered on that person's department, personal interests, and business objectives.

Next, you should try to identify the delta between skill sets that exist and those still needed. This is typically achieved over a series of casual conversations, but once people have told you what their department does and what it values, a reasonable question in the same conversation is to ask about the difference between what they seek and what they have, as it relates to current skills sets.

For example, you might ask: "Every business group experiences a difference between what is ideal versus what currently exists. Is that a challenge in your work area?"

Use your discretion choosing methods to build rapport. You will use the information you glean in later conversations.

Throughout these conversations, do not succumb to social convention that prevents us from revealing information about our unique abilities for fear it would be misinterpreted as egotistical—particularly if you're asked. At the same time, it's also important to recognize that not everyone has evolved to be comfortable doing this and hearing it from others.

2. Create a Skills Inventory

If your company does not utilize skills inventories as a process for staff development and succession planning, create your own. Compile a list of the skills that are necessary to perform your job well, and prioritize them in order of importance to the job.

For example, if you are an event planner, being well organized is a particularly important skill. If you are in sales, being able to clearly present a product's features and benefits is a valued skill. For those in product development, predicting market trends and generating innovative ideas are highly valued. Whatever your role, identify the top three skills necessary for success in that functional area.

Rate your competency against each of those skills, and for those where your competency level is less than excellent, propose ideas (training, independent projects, opportunities) that will enable you to improve that particular skill.

Segment your skills inventory into two parts:

- ▶ Skills that are valued and currently needed
- ▶ Skills that are not currently required, but are skills you possess that may have value in the future or in other areas of the business

3. Present Your Skills Inventory to Management

Meet with your manager and describe the concept of a skills inventory and how it can benefit the team. Explain how a plethora of skills exist across any given team; yet it is rare to put in place a structure and process that sets a blueprint to maximize efficient use of the team's aggregate skills.

Your meeting with management should not be an information dump. It should be grounded in the interests and specific needs of the business. Ask questions to establish relevance.

Meet with your manager to review the skills inventory you prepared. This is your opportunity to advance your career through well-structured productive advocacy.

Explain the purpose and the value of a skills inventory to give structure for your development as well as the development of others on the team.

Remember, the purpose of the skills inventory is to enable team members to promote their skills without appearing to be boastful or falling on the sword of humility.

As we evolve as humans, we may reach a point where social demands of humility and the insecurities and fear derived from competition will fall by the wayside. Until that time, we must advocate for ourselves and open opportunities that enable you to actively drive business success.

VALUING YOUR VALUE

Humility is clearly overrated when it inhibits the legitimate exchange of information about one's skills, abilities, and experiences that are relevant and valuable to the business. It is indisputable that there is a clear benefit in others learning the skills and values you bring to an organization and in your learning the skills and values of others.

The evolved leader should not fall victim to being driven by emotions and the natural human tendencies to acquiesce to people's feelings that inhibit this exchange. This knowledge transfer is paramount to your success.

Mastering the skill of productive advocacy can be a highly effective strategy for shifting into the fast lane of career success. Start today!

CHAPTER 7

Saving Face Versus Seeking Truth

"Go with your heart" and "Follow your gut" are expressions used interchangeably that serve as ill-directed guidance that, sadly, many people use in decision-making. Don't allow either of these to set the path of critical decision-making.

When people tell you, "Go with your heart," tell them your heart is as dumb as a sandbag when it comes to making critical decisions. Go with your brain.

For time ad infinitum, we've all heard the universal aphorism, and it has been useless for just about as long. My mother prided herself on the ability to sense the workings of the world seemingly based on nothing more than sniffing into the wind. Whether it was the motion of the clouds or some other ethereal indicator, she relied on her intuition with the same confidence I have with Google Maps for navigation.

If she were with us today, she would probably register her abilities in the app store for decision-making support. Sadly, her accuracy was a mere step up from random selection, no more reliable as rolling the dice. When she got it right, she would tout her "other-worldly" skills when, in fact, it was the result of drawing from unconscious data points in her brain that she simply didn't have the skill to bring to the forefront of her consciousness.

Many people believe there is something in the primordial soup of the cosmos that speaks to them. In reality, it's not the mystical soup driving their thinking; it's either sheer guesswork or the synapses firing in their brain unconsciously.

They call it intuition—the perceived ability to understand something instinctively without the need for conscious reasoning. However, it is far too mystical and unreliable to be a method for making the best business decisions affecting colleagues and the workplace.

Good decision-making must focus the lens on the data points and move them from the background of the unconscious to the forefront of clear vision. This translates directly to the workplace. I've had more bosses than I can count tell me "go with your gut" when they were unsure of a direction to take on a project.

I should have told my bosses, "Let's take a moment and carefully re-examine the options to decide which is the wiser direction to take." I didn't. You should.

Even as a child, I would wonder if my heart had some small, independent ganglion controlling my emotions. We associate the heart as the control center of our emotions but clearly no one changes who they love after having had a heart transplant. All emotions emanate from the brain. "Go with your heart" is simply a metaphor. Please relinquish control and defer your decision-making from "matters of the so-called heart" to conscious, analytical thinking of the brain.

Sometimes the "gut" we rely on obfuscates wisdom. The evolved leader jettisons reliance on the intangible. Hold the reins tightly. Steer your trajectory using intellect, logic, and reason One of the worst dangers of the so-called intuitive gut is that it is loaded with unconscious bias.

Many gut-based decisions result in exclusion of people based on appearance, religion, identity, or other dimensions of difference. These unwitting gut instincts mask destructive undercurrents of racism, sexism, and countless other unconscious biases that obstruct our ability to make wiser decisions. Starting today, muzzle your gut and get your brain to run the show. This is how decisions move in vastly more productive directions.

Sometimes the "gut" we rely on obfuscates wisdom.

There is a reason that the scientific method is used and works well. Decision-making centers on analyzing all available data points to determine the best logical steps to take.

The evolved leader carefully analyzes the data, the trajectory, and the facts. Use these as your guideposts for sound decision-making. I will briefly contradict myself. When you have fully exhausted all processes of intellect, logic, and reason, go ahead and use your gut.

There is an endless list of adages rooted to this illogical way of thinking. One particular comment that fuels my ire is, "Everything happens for a reason." This is most often used when someone has experienced something awful. I have heard people use that expression as a way to comfort the bereaved or for a wide range of unfortunate occurrences.

Shockingly, those who receive that message seem to be comforted. It truly rivals watching a magic show. You know what you just saw is impossible but somehow, oddly, walk away believing it. The expression is yet another example of how some people function in the world of the ill-defined.

What does the adage really mean when carefully analyzed? Did some high, omniscient spirit orchestrate the car crash with the intention of teaching someone a lesson? Instead, could it be saying that it was a terrible thing that happened, so don't wallow in it, make the best of it? The first interpretation implies that there was divine intervention and purpose beyond our ability to comprehend. This thinking may offer solace but little else. The focus on this issue is to highlight how common this practice is and how important it is to jettison.

A common thread woven throughout this book is the need to uncover and suppress our unconscious biases in decision-making. The evolved leader uses reason, logic, and intellect to make all decisions: acquiring talent, developing staff, motivating and inspiring, developing innovative products and services—literally dealing with all other aspects of managing a business or a team.

The best way to get to truth is to ask questions. Socrates made a career of this.

THE SOCRATIC VERSUS INSTRUCTIVE APPROACH TO CONFLICT RESOLUTION

A particularly innovative approach to uncovering logic and reason is rooted in ancient Greek philosophy. As far back as 450 BCE, the Athenian philosopher Socrates founded the concept of epistemology. The term comes from the ancient Greek *episteme*, meaning "knowledge," and the suffix *logi*, meaning "logical discourse." Socrates asked, "How do we know that we know?"

Much of Socrates's work focused on *a priori* and *a posteriori*. A priori knowledge is reached independently of direct experience (nonempirical) and relies on intuition or is arrived at beforehand, while a posteriori knowledge is based on direct experience (empirical or arrived at afterward).

Transcending all aspects of epistemology is the art and skill of asking questions. Sometimes these are closed-ended, typically binary or a limited number of choices. Or they are open-ended and require the respondent to elaborate. A core skill of evolved leadership is the ability to ask questions that enable others to provide comprehensive, well-thought-out answers based on logic and reasoning.

One of the most difficult tasks for any leader is the resolution of conflict, whether the conflict is between other colleagues or involves the leader directly. I recall speaking with one of the few female Fortune 500 CEOs. She shockingly told me that she doesn't experience any gender bias in the workplace. The look of amazement on my face caused her to smile and explain further.

A core skill of evolved leadership is the ability to ask questions that enable others to provide comprehensive, well-thought-out answers based on logic and reasoning.

She said: "I don't experience gender bias because I'm the CEO of one of the largest financial institutions in the country, and as a result, I'm always treated with the utmost respect and even deference. But when they don't know who I am, it rears its ugly head big time!"

She shared with me a story of attending a CEO conference. The conference was being held at a fancy resort, and spouses and partners were invited to attend. At the evening reception, couples were milling around. While standing alone, a prominent CEO approached and glanced at her name tag. As I'm sure many of you know, name tags at such events display the first name in much larger type than the last name. He looked up, and using her first name said, "That's a nice name. So, tell me, what company is your husband the CEO for?"

This female executive is the very definition of feisty, and what came next could likely have been a scene from *Game of Thrones*, and she was the dragon! With great pride, she repeated the five-minute diatribe she blasted at him, which began with "How dare you" and ended with "You need to move into the twenty-first century!"

In her raw style and with pride, she exclaimed, "I fixed his ass, right?!" She didn't get the affirmation she had expected from me. The rest of the conversation focused on my recommendation to apply the Socratic versus instructive approach to conflict resolution for a far more productive outcome.

I explained, her chastisement was expertly instructional but was void of the Socratic. Several months passed before we saw each other again. Even before offering a greeting, she declared that what we had discussed had changed everything. She recounted, "I came across someone else who assumed I was the spouse, and my husband was the CEO. This time I did exactly what you advised with that Socratic versus instructive thing. I simply asked, 'How did you come to the conclusion that my husband was the CEO and I was the spouse?'"

Realizing his mistake, he apologized, started retreating backwards. She didn't let him off the hook and called him back, "It might seem obvious," she said, "but I'd really like to just walk through the process. Tell me, how did you come to that conclusion?"

Because that Socratic approach was nonaccusatory, he had to contemplate the underlying reason for his assumption and was compelled to state what seemed the obvious. "I guess I assumed that, because you're a woman."

The smile on the face of this normally very cynical CEO told the story. She said, "He got it! Unlike that other guy who just wanted to get away from 'that woman' who had steam coming out of my ears, this guy *really* got it. I could tell he will never do it again."

Not under duress, but because he genuinely understood the logic and reason behind his actions.

The evolved leader recognizes that chastising, scolding, or instructing people on how they should behave sometimes gets them to take the actions you direct but will be done only under duress or being muzzled. The goal must be to gain understanding and *buy-in* because they understand the benefit and reason. It is the Socratic approach that facilitates this effectively.

When the conflict involves a power differential, things can inhibit the Socratic process. A pervasive cloud that flows through many workplace cultures is "Don't cross the boss!" There are many halls of industry paved with the bones of those who did and failed.

Many bosses are only too thrilled to be flattered by team members who smile and agree with their brilliant insight and vision. This often is a mask that hides an undercurrent of disagreement. Their congenial smiles, nods, and grins are the product of something called "MicroDeceptions."

This is the more complicated gray area where gut reaction and logic overlap. Instinct tells you to not cross the boss, while logic tells you conditions will never change if they are not addressed. These MicroDeceptions represent the unfortunate channel where the boss can become the real victim.

MICRODECEPTIONS AND THE HALO EFFECT

On the bumpy road to great leadership, we encounter the good, the bad, and the invisible.

More often, the good and the bad are easily observed and managed. The invisible behaviors tend not to present themselves in such clear and tangible forms. They often go undetected, doing insidious harm with no knowledge of how the damage occurred. Exposure to these is not unlike the invisible power of radiation and can be exceptionally damaging—not just for those who are being managed but for leaders, as well.

In a strange twist to the standard, top-down flow of leadership protocol that focuses on the role of managers in uncovering and developing the skills of their teams, let me add MicroDeceptions to the mix.

In the world of sending subtle messages (micromessaging) there are MicroInequities and MicroAdvantages. MicroInequities are subtle, semiconscious messages sent differently to different individuals or groups that impair a recipient's performance. MicroAdvantages are subtle messages, often sent consciously, to those we admire and respect that motivate, inspire, and encourage them to aspire to great levels. MicroInequities tend to impair the performance of their recipients on all levels of the organizational hierarchy.

MicroDeceptions, however, represent a reversal of this flow and place the greatest impediment on those with more power and control. One doesn't typically think of the boss as a victim. Yet these pernicious messages are unwittingly sent by subordinates to their superiors. Do subordinates agree with the boss because they've concluded that the boss's idea is the best one, or are they just been influenced by the source of the idea? Ultimately, MicroDeceptions limit and encumber the performance of both parties.

MicroDeceptions can be quite powerful and ubiquitous, even at the C-suite level, and they almost always have a profound impact on one's leadership success.

I recall giving a keynote to an executive vice president and his senior management team at the leading computer chip manufacturing company. During the break, he privately asked me, "Do you think, at my level, I ever get any MicroInequities?" My response was a resounding no! "At your level," I said, "people don't typically receive MicroInequities. People are cautious about offending the boss. It's more likely that you receive MicroDeceptions."

I could see the wheels spinning, and the expression on his face said it all. He could sense where this was going, and all his antennae had tuned to full alert. He reeled back, asking, "What exactly are MicroDeceptions, and why would I be getting them?"

I shared that MicroDeceptions mean, you as the leader, never know when you're hearing the truth. As a senior leader, when people communicate with you, respond to your comments, or just listen to you speak, they often send back messages that are filtered through caution motivated by self-preservation and not necessarily truth. This brought him to a full stop.

It's important to understand that these untruthful messages are not sent with malicious intent. The phenomenon occurs for one of two reasons:

- ▶ Self-preservation (job security)
- ▶ Blind admiration (the halo effect)

People are careful not to offend those who control their destiny and job security. The aphorism "Don't poke the bear" comes into play. Or people are influenced by the stature and assumed wisdom bestowed upon the boss's position of high esteem. This is known as the "halo effect" or "white coat syndrome."

It's no secret that people are hesitant to disagree with or challenge the boss. It's safer to stroke the boss's ego and preserve one's job security and career trajectory. This is particularly complex and layered when DEI differences are factored in.

The halo effect operates in the realm of the invisible. It's common that people laugh at the boss's joke—even when it's not funny. I'm sure everyone has sat in a meeting where the boss said something intended to be humorous and the entire conference room cackles, as if he or she were headlining at Caroline's Comedy Club in Times Square.

On the other hand, if someone else were to utter the very same remark, it would likely be received with a sigh, roll of the eyes, and headshake of dismissal. Funny thing—under the halo effect, people actually deceive *themselves* into genuinely believing that the boss's joke was, in truth, the height of humor.

After sharing all this, the window fully opened for this EVP. He realized he had no confidence that what he was hearing was what people actually felt and believed about his ideas and vision.

Bottom line: Undetected MicroDeceptions block both truth and organizational performance. Most critically, the outcome of this behavior is that the recipient of MicroDeceptions is likely not getting the team's best thinking, perspectives, insights, and contributions.

"Wait a minute," he responded defensively. "I always ask my people to tell me what they really think. Isn't that enough?" That question became the impetus for a two hour executive coaching session following the meeting. Here are some of the highlights.

Simply asking people to tell you what they think is well intended but is not enough. The flaw is that merely inviting challenge doesn't offer the safe haven to do so. Don't just invite people to challenge your perspective; make it a requirement.

I shared with him a technique I first used early in my career as a middle manager on Wall Street. I kicked off one of my staff meetings, saying, "There are ten of us on this team, the nine of you and one of me. That's not a qualitative comment, just a numerical data point. If your perspective always agrees with mine, then we don't need you, except to complete busy work and mundane tasks. It lessens your value to the team."

I explained, "You were all hired for your thinking capacity. I expect to tap into that to bring different perspectives and viewpoints to everything we do. It doesn't mean that I will always agree with and accept those perspectives—but I do require them from you."

**Don't just invite people to challenge
your perspective; make it a requirement.**

To ensure that this directive would go from a request to a requirement, I informed the members of the team that their performance appraisals, as well as my endorsement for future opportunities, would hinge largely on demonstrating innovative and challenging thinking as a cornerstone of making our team more effective.

A secondary and equally critical step for leaders is to never be defensive or dismissive of any challenge offered. It is *essential* that

you explore different perspectives thoroughly and express appreciation of their value.

This process resonated deeply for that executive. He was quite
forthcoming in acknowledging that he had always been more comfortable with compliance and confirmation of his thinking than the
vulnerability to his image of not having all the answers.

Several months later, he reached out to me. He confessed that
although these concepts and skills had not been in his comfort zone,
he did see their value. Most importantly, when he applied them, he
saw a clear and measurable difference in performance levels and the
ways his team operated.

Here's what he did.

When presenting to his entire business unit of several hundred
employees about a new product release, he asked the audience for
input on the product strategy. He heard nothing more than pandering responses such as, "The only problem I see is that we should have
released this sooner," and "Why do we have to wait until next month
to talk about this with our clients?"

He said to me, "The window had opened, and I saw these as
MicroDeceptions and brown-nosing responses." He genuinely
applied the concepts and told the group that there are hundreds
of great thinking minds among them. Someone among the hundreds of people here today must see something we could have done
or should do differently to make it better! After a brief silence, one
brave soul stood up and challenged the absence of a particular feature the employee felt would make the product more desirable and
make it distinctly more competitive.

He applied the technique perfectly, beginning his response by
thanking the employee for being direct and offering his insight. He
took it one step further by saying, "It's people like you I really value
and I thank you for challenging this." He went on to ask a series of
clarifying questions and ended the exchange by thanking him again
and reiterating how much he values input from those who challenge
the status quo.

He said, "It was like a floodgate had opened. People seemed to come out of the woodwork with ideas and constructive criticism. Most importantly, they weren't doing it just for sport. The comments were genuinely valuable." The culture had shifted.

The skills and techniques for avoiding MicroDeceptions had now been infused into their culture. He and other managers had virtually extinguished MicroDeceptions and their ill effect within their respective workplace cultures and had created an environment of productive psychological safety.

IT'S NOT ALWAYS TOP DOWN

One of our company seminars focuses exclusively on the broader mission of minimizing inhibition and maximizing the freedom to contribute in the workplace. This goes a step beyond MicroDeceptions and includes building the skills that encourage all employees to feel safe in challenging thinking across all disciplines and levels. This safe haven is universally known as "psychological safety" and was introduced earlier in Chapter 4 on connective language as an essential part of Tier 3 behavior.

Psychological Safety

Psychological safety is that part of a corporate culture mission that enables people in the workplace to feel unencumbered, uninhibited, and able to speak and share their thoughts freely.

The mission is to create team cultures that foster not only ethnic, gender, and other diversity within the workplace, but also diversity of thought through open and honest communication.

Cultivating an environment where all people feel safe to bring their full selves to work and speak freely without fear of retribution is inextricably linked to workplace performance.

To achieve a psychologically safe workplace, colleagues must first master the skills of identifying MicroInequities and ensuring the messages that they send support an authentic platform of psychological safety. This sits at the root of the solution.

Typically, lack of psychological safety is not the result of blatant or conscious bad behavior. These messages tend to be subtle and inadvertent. They are expressed through looks, gestures, tone of voice, and other forms. These subtle signals often cause colleagues who receive them to question their personal value and ultimately influence their commitment to a team or a company.

Instinctively, people have a burning drive to be right. We look for confirmation of our beliefs from others. Evolved leaders are those who learn the greater value in seeking truth over being right. It is impossible to achieve a psychologically safe work environment until we learn how to prevent our egos from inhibiting the pursuit of collaboration.

The launch of any project needs to establish a clear set of performance expectations and well-defined objectives and outcomes. As an evolved leader, you are responsible for ensuring that the members of your team know their key role of bringing creativity, innovation, and insight to enhance the success of every project in which they participate. Reaching this performance level requires the elimination of MicroDeceptions to open a broad, two-way swinging door for the best possible team performance. People are hired for their thinking capacity. How could anyone be a great leader if they don't tap the great minds of the people with whom they work?

Practice these key steps to accomplish an open, genuine dialogue and exchange of ideas:

- ▶ Don't simply invite opinions that differ from yours. Make it a requirement.
- ▶ Never respond to a challenge with a statement. Always ask a clarifying question.
- ▶ Elaborate on what was said to show your understanding.
- ▶ If you disagree, outline your concerns and ask how the person would address them.

▶ Solicit feedback from others present.
▶ Accept or reject the challenge with a clear explanation, not a declaration.
▶ Whether accepted or not, express appreciation for people having offered their challenging perspective.

CHAPTER 8

The Paradox of Political Correctness

OTHER VERSUS LESSER

"Shame on you! How dare you make that person feel like an 'Other.'"

If you've spent any time in the corporate workplace, it's likely you've heard this or some similar scolding, about making someone feel like an Other. This advice stems from the ever-vigilant world of political correctness (PC).

Most workplaces have an unlimited supply of kid gloves available for managing the PC world. When it seems you might be putting your hands on something that's socially risky, there are plenty of folks who will toss a pair your way to help avoid offending or hurting someone's feelings. The gloves are also donned as protection against the even higher risk of litigation.

The underlying motivation is well intentioned but may prove toxic by unwittingly pulling you into regressive leadership. If the goal is to move culture forward and bring disenfranchised people to a level of equity, shouldn't we strive to highlight people's differences as an asset? Shouldn't we acknowledge their value and appreciate what their difference brings to the vitality of the business, rather than safely steering clear? Anything less than this would be regressive leadership and counter to the mission of workplace inclusion.

As with most things in the world, it's not so much the "what," but the "how" that matters. Avoidance is *never* the better option to resolve any point of tension. Stepping up to an issue is more difficult and certainly uncomfortable, but infinitely wiser and more productive.

Clients have told me of the many times they've been chastised by colleagues when they've asked about someone's difference. It's the old, "Shame on you!" It's become a ubiquitous admonishment, in the spirit of diversity, equity, and inclusion—but the paradox is palpable and couldn't be more counter to the stated mission.

How could anyone be upset when the behavior springs from an Eden garden of good intentions? Why would we ever want someone to be made to feel left out or not a part of the team? The flaw is that we've come to associate the term "other" as a pejorative. In today's business vernacular, Other carries a negative connotation. This is a misguided thinking. "Other" means just that: not the same.

In truth, Other is a powerful asset. Where the spheres of diverse backgrounds and experience intersect, innovative ideas and solutions emerge.

So why do we caution our colleagues to avoid addressing the differences that distinguish us and fuel diversity of thought? Why do we consider such acknowledgment an act of insensitivity or divisiveness? It is a path driven by the pressures of political correctness.

One of the most unfortunate mantras of the PC world is, "Better safe than sorry," When we avoid another person's otherness, in an attempt to respect the person, it creates a paradox. That avoidance and overcompensation become potentially detrimental to the original mission of inclusiveness. The attempt to blanket bad behavior ends up obfuscating what is potentially beneficial to the mission.

Such avoidance is actually counter to the primary objective of valuing and harnessing our differences to achieve a competitive advantage. It fosters a culture that enriches employee experience and strengthens business outcomes. What a peculiar paradox, indeed! How can we ever appreciate those differences if we don't acknowledge their existence?

> **Where the spheres of diverse backgrounds and experience intersect, innovative ideas and solutions emerge.**

The primary mission of inclusion is to bring together the powerful mosaic of those differences to support higher levels of creativity, innovation, insight, and productivity. Failing to acknowledge the differences of others pretty much ensures casting ourselves as lead characters in a reboot of *The Emperor's New Clothes*! So what the heck are we supposed to do?

Admittedly, there are insensitive and offensive ways to address such issues, and we certainly wouldn't advocate prancing in a field of those social landmines. It's only when the connotation makes the person feel "lesser than" that it becomes a problem. Let's change the landscape of behavior and strive toward making it clear that respectful inquiries or acknowledgment that someone is different becomes linked with highlighting their value.

Other Is Good—Lesser Than Is Bad

There is a vast difference between "Other" and "Lesser Than." Although simplistic in structure, the terminology influences the actions we take. When we are motivated by avoidance of difference, we lose the benefits of workplace inclusion. On the other hand, when our motivation seeks to acknowledge and value difference, we step into the fast lane, propelling a work culture forward.

As I travel the world, my visually obvious Otherness is frankly invigorating and invites rich discussion and discovery. Conversely, I have also experienced being treated as both an interesting Other and a Lesser Than.

As an American, I have been made to feel unwelcome, excluded, and even ostracized, solely based on my nationality. It isn't the sort of thing that's hard to detect once people hear me speak. They are quickly able to detect I'm an American. Although, unspoken, their thoughts are audible—"That's an American!" The stereotypes of the "ugly American" are conjured, and sentiments manifest in a tone of disdain. When this happens, the effect on me is palpable. My motivation to engage is extinguished and unconscious defensive countermeasures are launched. The result; the meeting becomes tainted for both sides.

I was being judged based on my affiliation with preconceived notions of a national profile for which they held high disapproval. That Otherness became an unwarranted trigger for becoming a Lesser Than. All too often, these triggers are without logic or merit. It became evident that the Lesser Than micromessages I received were based on those preconceived judgments. There was an elephant in the room, and the only way to evict him was to first place him squarely in the center of the table and address his presence head-on.

I paused the meeting and in Socratic style redirected the discussion to this unspoken issue. I said, "I couldn't help but notice that I seem to be getting different messages than those being sent to others in our meeting."

Of course, the people in the meeting feigned blindness to the difference in treatment. So I moved to the next stage. In unemotional, tangible, and clear terms, I identified the specific behaviors I had observed, describing the differences in eye contact, tone of voice, and even subtle headshaking to convey disagreement even before my ideas had been expressed. I wrapped it up by describing how these micromessages were sent differently to me than to other members in the group. I had shone a spotlight with clear evidence of having received treatment that was lesser than, presumably based on my difference. This approach facilitated meaningful discussion.

Although people didn't fall on their sword, they did want to save face, and the interaction noticeably improved through the balance of the meeting.

People are often too embarrassed or timid to admit to their inequitable bad behavior based on someone's Otherness. But by simply making them aware of the impact of their unspoken micromessages, that elephant often makes its way to the door and exits the building—and in this case, it did.

Where Are You From?

All that being said, there is a particular sensitivity when approaching someone about their difference when that trait touches a sensitive nerve. In the United States, some cultural groups (Latinos, Middle Easterners, and others) have been marginalized based on political and/or religious beliefs. They are sometimes more easily identified by their style of dress or accent. Some of these groups have been routine recipients of exclusionary behavior. Their differences may spark actions by some that put them at risk for investigation or deportation. Merely having a Spanish accent in a US border city could result in a call to Immigration and Customs Enforcement.

For this reason, a simple "Where are you from?" can be a particularly sensitive question for a Latino. The question could be interpreted as a genuine interest in getting to know someone, with a different culture being just one aspect of building rapport; or the inference could become a "lesser-than" question suggesting, "You sound like you might be here illegally."

One approach embraces the person's difference, while the other carries a nefarious, accusatory undertone. Those same four words—"Where are you from?"—can carry vastly different meanings.

Being an African American stopped by the police is a difference that sometimes goes beyond Other and slides down the slippery slope into Lesser Than in potentially catastrophic ways.

For African Americans, Latinos, Middle Easterners, Sikhs, and many other groups, there is a heightened sensitivity, as their difference is often the first thing one sees. These groups are proud of their differences. But their antennae have been tuned to messages of exclusion and disrespect.

Another cohort for which one should use careful discretion is people with disabilities. In this case, asking about someone's disability should probably not be the first topic of discussion upon meeting the person. Only after getting to know them and establishing a clear foundation of respect and engagement, could one open that door. One approach might be, "In working together, we've learned a fair amount about each other over our time as colleagues, and I'd appreciate getting to know you better. Would you be comfortable talking about workplace disabilities and how they might, or might not, affect the ways people interact with you?"

As an evolved leader, you must make it clear that your interest is in building a culture that embraces the team's differences and values those differences as assets.

I was in a restaurant with a family member who was observing my casual exchange with the waiter. He had a noticeably strong accent that appeared to have traces of Eastern European influence.

We were having a pleasant exchange during which I said, "I'm hearing something in your voice that sounds Eastern European. Where are you from?" With a proud and pleasant smile, he answered, "Slovakia." He mentioned he'd been in this country for six years and shared a brief story of what brought him to America along with his dream of becoming a film producer. There was no confusion what those four words were pleasantly conveying.

This was reminiscent of countless conversations I've had over the years with people in the United States where it seemed easy to detect what appeared to be a nonnative speaker. It was a marvelous model of what we claim diversity should truly be all about—welcoming and appreciating our many cultural differences and experiences.

Being particularly sensitive, my family member challenged the appropriateness of posing that question to the waiter. She had a heightened sense of cultural and political correctness and said, "I was surprised that you, as an expert in culture and inclusion, would ask such an inappropriate question of someone you don't know." She suggested that asking people where they're from may cause them to feel like an Other, implying, of course, that Other was a bad thing. The admonishment was reminiscent of countless conversations I've had over the years when noticing a discernible accent.

Hearing her concern, I asked a fundamental question: "How would my question cause a problem for the waiter?"

She responded, saying, "This would make him feel marginalized as an Other."

I then asked, "Is being Other inherently a bad thing?"

I continued with more Socratic questioning in which I was careful not to malign her position but instead challenged her to explain the risks versus the benefits of sending messages of inquiry and engagement.

I explained that my conversation with the waiter was a marvelous model. It demonstrated the aspiration and value of diversity. The waiter clearly decoded the positive intent of my message and appreciated my interest in getting to know him.

Let's stop and take a brief step back from this scenario to examine how one should best respond to challenge. This is one of the cornerstones of becoming an evolved leader.

▶ Your first response should always end with a question mark.
▶ Never respond defensively to any challenge.
▶ Always ask qualifying questions.

The evolved leader doesn't battle; the evolved leader seeks truth. When responding with a defensive statement, the challenger is put in a defensive position. No matter how strong your position may be and no matter how uncomfortable you may find it, never respond with a condemnation or putdown. Require people to explain the underlying logic of their position—which is often as simple as asking, "Tell me more?"

It's a powerful technique that defuses conflict and invites engagement, particularly when there are strong differences of opinion.

Without question, that waiter did feel like an Other—but in the best possible sense! The connotation of my micromessages rose above any uncertainty. Through my tone of voice and facial expression, he instinctively knew that my question was a bridge of connection and not a statement of judgment.

Other is the fertile ground that generates new ideas, perspectives, solutions, and actions that ignite business growth and success.

Fears about political correctness sometimes derail what might otherwise be well-intended messages. How many times have you heard someone say, "You had better not say that because you'll probably get into trouble." The term "political correctness" has become a euphemism for unnecessary overreaction. It has fallen into the social protocol folder, where it recently has been joined by "wokeness." When carefully examined, political correctness suggests being on the front burner of guidelines that define acceptable and unacceptable behavior in the workplace. How could anything that's "correct" be wrong?

Other is the fertile ground that generates new ideas, perspectives, solutions, and actions that ignite business growth and success.

Although the title of this chapter is "The Paradox of Political Correctness," in fact, political correctness is not paradoxical. Again, if something is correct, then how can it be wrong? And whether in a political context or any other social arena, if it is, in fact, correct, then one should proudly embrace it.

Making an offensive comment about someone's appearance isn't politically correct, not because it's an overreaction, but because it's simply wrong. Using a racial epithet, treating women inequitably, or having a different standard of behavior based on someone's sexual identity is not a matter of political correctness; it is simply wrong.

The evolved leader must be the voice that speaks up in recognition of what is fundamentally right and never allow behavior that is wrong to be justified under a derogatory moniker of political correctness.

DENOTATION VERSUS CONNOTATION

Pay particular attention to the denotation versus connotation of your messages. Denotation is about words—their definitions and the precision of their meaning. Connotation is what reveals the message we are actually conveying. Connotation always rules. It's all about what we are actually saying regardless of the actual words themselves.

Connotation is interpreted through tone, nuance, inflection, facial expressions, inference, syntax, and the framing of your words that reveal their true meaning and intent. Denotation pales by comparison.

In the case of the waiter, he read the connotation of my message perfectly. He knew I was genuinely interested in and respectful of his difference—we were cool.

Clarity of our messages is a cornerstone of great leadership. This is not just about feelings. This is about performance. Political correctness can sometimes force denotation to fit into the parameters of a social formula or checklist of expectations. All too often, the checklist is executed well, but the message fuels distance.

It is not politically correct for someone to call me a jerk. I can assure you though, when I call my dear nephew, with whom I have a very tight bond of safety and love, a jerk, he knows—through my playful tone, smile, and arm around his shoulder—that the connotation is sending a clear message of caring and love.

In the leadership world, our connotation does more than merely cause someone to feel like an Other or Lesser Than. It forges an understanding of respectful engagement and influences loyalty and performance.

Recognizing someone's difference as a potential asset motivates and enables people to perform to their fullest potential.

For some, this might sound a bit Panglossian. But not everyone's idea is necessarily a good one. Some ideas are simply flat-out bad. It's not whether the idea is good or bad. It's all about the method and process you use to determine its value that *defines* your effectiveness as a leader. Sadly, the methods we use to determine value can be tainted by the profile of the person who offers the idea.

We all harbor internal sentiments toward different groups. Instinct can cause some to be drawn to those who share our beliefs, interests, values, and ethnic profiles. For some, however, there is a draw toward beliefs and profiles that starkly counter their own. All of us have some degree of interest or attraction to opposites. The interest ranges from distant curiosity to allure and magnetism. Science rests on the cardinal belief of pursuing all possibilities in researching a topic. The scientific method is the more logical approach. It doesn't value our personal feelings and biases. It only seeks the facts. Regrettably, maybe even disastrously, people fall victim to more shallow, primal, instinctive feelings and build walls of resistance.

Sometimes these impenetrable walls become the building blocks of our "isms."

THE SEGMENTATION OF "ISMS"

We all know that rejection of a group of people, based on their profile, is inherently bad. No one wants to be perceived as a racist, sexist, xenophobe, nationalist, supremacist, or any of the multitude of other "ists," "isms," or "phobes" that represent the filtering process of our biases that undermine the rights of others.

Now more than ever, we need to gain a stronger grasp around the roots of this filtering process. Understanding the segmentation of our isms enables us to manage and mitigate them more effectively. Our global isms generally fall into one or more of four basic segments:

- ▶ Axiom-ism
- ▶ Power-ism
- ▶ Class-ism
- ▶ Opportune-ism

Let's take a closer look at each.

Axiom-ism

In mathematics an axiom is an unprovable assumption of fact. Social axioms represent our core beliefs of right and wrong; unlike math and logic, we often hold steadfast to the assumptions that they do represent ultimate rightness and wrongness with the same confidence. These axioms relate closely to the deontological branch of ethics—the belief that basic axioms of right and wrong exist independent of consequences.

A person holding onto an axiom thinks along these lines: "Anyone who is incapable of seeing my view is foolish or mistaken. Those who believe the world is flat are idiots. You don't deserve my respect, and I seek to change your foolish belief."

A social axiom can also imply that any opposing view needs to be changed to coincide with the axiom. This concept is most compelling in the way it manifests through religious beliefs, gender orientation, and political parties.

Power-ism

There are also biases guided by our innate desire for power and control. They manifest as looking down on those who don't have "matching stripes." They are revealed in domination via hierarchy, wealth, title, and industry affiliation.

The root cause of gender bias and gender discrimination originates in the power-ism of physical size. The practice is universal and has been a part of our sociology throughout human history. Whether in religious texts or as far back as our Neanderthal beginnings, men have been in control because they have the physical power advantage. If, from the beginning, women were on average 6 inches taller, 50 pounds heavier, and had 30 percent more muscle mass, it would be highly questionable whether this power disparity would be so prevalent. Frankly, it would likely not exist.

Whether through the process of electing political representatives or through succession planning for senior executives, even among men, the taller person is almost always chosen. This is why the challenge in achieving gender balance is so difficult. Men will always have a larger physical stature over women. The one exception is succession within monarchies; there, physical size hasn't mattered.

Class-ism

Class-ism is the most dominant and influential of the four segments of isms. It is fundamentally manifested in the belief that "I am better than you." I am better educated, I am more widely read, I have a superior mastery of the language and vocabulary, I am more well traveled, smarter, and generally more worldly; therefore, I feel it is appropriate to treat those who are not my equals in ways that reinforce my superiority—usually done subtly through micromessages. Classism is the primary cause of today's racism.

Consider the example of the woman in Central Park who called the police on the African American birdwatcher. Had she known that this Black man was a Harvard University graduate, a member of the Board of Directors of the Audubon Society, and the recipient of other esteemed accolades, that knowledge would likely have resulted in a very different course of action. Knowing his *class* affiliation, it would likely never have resulted in her placing that 911 emergency call to the police.

In the legal arena, many Black defense attorneys, men and women, report being mistakenly chastised by the judge when seated alone at the defense table because they are mistaken for the criminal defendant. The common scolding is, "You shouldn't be sitting there until your attorney shows up." Once the attorney clarifies the error, it is often met with a nervous laugh and glossed over. This would, of course, never occur in the reverse.

In a study conducted in the early 1990s, during the peak of *The Cosby Show*, people who acknowledged they were racist were asked if Dr. Huxtable, his attorney wife, and their children moved into your neighborhood, would they be opposed to it? More than half the respondents reported they would be comfortable having them as neighbors. Ultimately, it had less to do with their race and more about class affiliation.

Race functions as nothing more than a label, and not core opposition to their genealogy. Within the *Classism* sector there is the subset of *Familiarity*. It has the power to dissipate other biases. If it is determined that you are one of my "people," then I will naturally find, or even make excuses for, your inclusion and acceptance.

Opportune-ism

Opportune-ism is bias driven by the pursuit of personal gain at the expense of others—it targets anyone. Race, gender, identity, or other profile differences play no role and have no bearing on a person's actions of bias. It simply boils down to basic predator practice where one takes advantage of easy prey. For an opportunist, if taking advantage will help achieve personal gain, then the attack is launched.

In the workplace, it would be unusual to malign or take advantage of colleagues who are the boss's known favorites. Opportunism is one of the most challenging biases to confront. In one multinational company, the CEO's nephew was marginally qualified for the job he held. When a higher-level position became available, he threw his hat in the ring, along with several others who were demonstrably better qualified for the job. Although the better-qualified candidates were hopeful that nepotism would not interfere, no one risked shining a light on the shortcomings of the CEO's nephew, fearing repercussions from several levels above. He got the job. The nephew shamelessly exploited his relationship and vanquished weaker prey. In some cases, knowledge is power, but sometimes, in the words of Cersei Lannister, queen of House Lannister, "Power is power." In this case, the CEO's nephew consciously leveraged his advantage at the cost of the company and others.

Conversely, it's not uncommon for people to jump on the bandwagon of condescension when those who are respected speak disparagingly about a colleague. Keep friends in high places, and watch your back, or you may fall victim to the opportunist. Tragically, in the workplace, those who are perceived as weak prey are disproportionately aligned with race and gender.

INTERSECTIONALITY

Let's not overlook intersectionality. Although not an ism directly, it is closely aligned. Coined by Professor Kimberlé Crenshaw, the term "intersectionality" is defined as the interconnected nature of social categorizations such as race, class, gender, and others as they apply to a given individual or group, creating an overlapping of discrimination or disadvantage.

Intersectionality is having representation from multiple ism segments. For example, a disabled, Black, Muslim female is likely to experience a compounded effect, based on her myriad segmentations of isms. In managing these inhibiting forces that directly impact workplace performance, we will be more effective at achieving meaningful change when we better understand the root causes.

The evolved leader doesn't merely dictate a set of prescribed behaviors—this accomplishes little more than muzzling people. The effective coaching of behavior requires bringing people to a level of greater consciousness of the reasons for their actions.

CULTURAL EQUITY TEAMS

Attempts to remedy the inhibiting effects of isms are seemingly endless. One broad-scale approach has been the proverbial Employee Resource Groups (ERGs). Over the years, these employee organizations have created safe havens and solace for many marginalized employees who share common demographic and cultural profiles. While they served an important purpose at their inception and have done great work infusing diverse perspectives into workplace culture, the question today is whether they are keeping pace with a rapidly evolving, multicultural, and intersectional landscape.

As workplace culture advances, has the effectiveness of ERGs diminished? Has the time come for a seismic shift in structure to ensure a continuation of positive culture change and organizational evolution?

If these organizations fail to stay in touch with the forward momentum of business, they run the risk of slipping into stasis, irrelevance, or decline. If you fail to evolve, you will diminish.

For their members, ERGs were comforting because of shared workplace challenges and obstacles. They have stagnated into divisive social silos. Instead, this structure should reinforce the opposite. Silos should be jettisoned, and ERGs should come together as *one* business group to pursue a common set of objectives.

This was strikingly illustrated for me when being chastised by a transgender woman toward the end of a seminar during the Q&A. She first expressed her appreciation for the strategies and techniques presented during the session but then shifted to express disappointment in me for not having addressed the issues of transgenderism. She became quite emotional about how important this issue was to her and other people who shared her identity profile.

My response laid out the clear difference between current DEI philosophy and where it needs to evolve. I explained that there would be no problem for me to detail the stages of transgenderism, from the initial certification of one's identity through full affirmation and transition.

The cornerstone question I asked her was, "If everyone here were to leave this session with a full understanding of the challenges surrounding transgender life, how would you want them to treat you differently in their next meeting with you, or when they wrote their next email, or in discussing a project with you? What specifically should they do differently with their new knowledge?"

She sat silently for a moment. I offered, "I think the answer is, you don't want anyone to focus on your difference or profile, you just don't want them to treat you differently based on that difference." She agreed.

The goal should not be to manage checklists of the different ways people should treat various profiled groups. Instead, we must develop the skills to send messages that demonstrate equity, respect, and inclusion consistently for all—and strive for equitable engagement, so that all aspects of the ways we communicate exude appreciation, respect, and value across all groups and dimensions equitably.

In line with this vision, we reengineered and introduced a new infrastructure in place of the traditional ERGs called cultural equity teams (CETs). Intersectional and positioned to accomplish a collective set of common business objectives, CETs jettison the old siloed ERGs. They replace them with a stronger, more influential, unified, DEI business collaborative. For companies that have embraced this approach, the impact has been seismic and has ignited a cascade of change.

Unlike the ERG, the CET is not a social group, safe haven, or venting platform for its members. Instead, the CET is configured for fostering collaboration and contribution to the business and being a true catalyst for change. It is far better positioned to support the demands of both the current and future workplace than traditional affinity groups.

CHAPTER 9

Value Protocols

Corporate operating principles have become a staple within businesses across all industries for decades. They take on the form of statements that define a set of expectations relating to the standards for working internally with colleagues and externally with customers, media, and others.

These precepts, often prominently displayed throughout a company's corridors and websites, take on a range of monikers, including "Corporate Value Statements," "Operating Principles," "Mission Statements," and more.

Businesses can be quite creative in the formatting used to convey these statements. They can be as crisp as a simple list of single-word declarations:

- ▸ Excellence
- ▸ Quality
- ▸ Consistency
- ▸ Teamwork

Or catchy platitudes like:

- ▸ Customers First
- ▸ Respect for the Individual
- ▸ Integrity Above All

These declarations sometimes also include brief descriptions to provide clarity and guidance.

Some companies are quite detailed in the structure and communication of their operating principles. For example, defense contractors often publish detailed brochures setting very clear protocols and expectations of conduct, including illustrations that leave no room for misinterpretation or uncertainty. They seek to avoid any risk to the stability of their government contracts.

Whatever form they take, corporate values serve a critical need. They strive to define a corporate culture and identify the behaviors required to support it. Value statements establish what a business requires from its employees in the ways needed to fulfill the corporate cultural ethic.

If establishing these protocols is a worthwhile process for a business, why shouldn't this extend to each of us as individuals, as well? Don't we all have our own code of ethics that we subscribe to and would advocate from others?

This chapter establishes the rationale for extending this practice beyond the very high-level corporate protocols of behavior required of all employees, right down to our individual and team expectations.

We call these individual operating principles "value protocols."

Value protocols are the set of behaviors that define your personal values, combined with effective strategies (protocols) that help the business operate more productively and make you a more effective colleague and leader. When leaders establish and apply a set of value protocols, the impact on performance can be transformative.

These protocols are a set of standards that don't change based on changing conditions or circumstances. Just as companies create operating principles and value statements that are meant to endure through all types of change, so too should evolved leaders implement value protocols for themselves and their teams.

Value protocols differ from personal values in that personal values represent the things we subscribe to and believe in the ways we manage our lives. Whereas value protocols represent a set of professional procedures we commit to that may have no relation to our personal views.

They seek to create guideposts where everyone can perform to their highest potential. They are designed to provide effective strategies that make a business operate more productively and make you a more effective colleague and leader.

Value protocols are not effective if they remain cerebral and you keep them to yourself. You must present value protocols to those with whom you work and gain their agreement on the benefit and value of making them an integral part of how you collaborate as a team.

> **Just as companies create operating principles and value statements that are meant to endure through all types of change, so too should evolved leaders implement value protocols for themselves and their teams.**

Here are some recommended value protocols upon which you can build that can transform the thought process of an entire team. More importantly, they instill new ways of thinking that can be converted into higher performance. You can take these in the form presented here or adapt them to align with your professional values.

Value Protocols

1. Require every criticism to include a recommendation.
2. Start with "Yes."
3. Always ask meeting attendees for input and perspective.
4. Ensure timely distribution of information .
5. Routinely provide developmental feedback.
6. Start broadly.
7. Don't wait—initiate.
8. Listen with the intent of understanding.
9. Validate—don't speculate.

Let's take a closer look at what each value protocol means and how to apply it.

1. REQUIRE EVERY CRITICISM TO INCLUDE A RECOMMENDATION

Whining, complaining, or criticizing is a routine way people express sentiments of opposition or discontent in the workplace. Frankly, it's as common as a yawn and all too often gets the same response— nothing. There is awareness but no action taken.

Recognizing that a problem exists or criticizing the status quo should never be good enough. This first value protocol establishes the practice that every criticism should immediately be followed with a recommended solution. Require this!

Let's look at some examples.

I was sharing some of our value protocol concepts with the CEO of a major technology company. He asked me to sit in on one of his upcoming staff meetings and present the concepts to his executive team.

Following that presentation, the discussion shifted to a different area of leadership development. One executive complained that he had not been made aware of an organizational change and spent a full minute talking about how often information is learned through back channels and even from third parties such as news media. He ended his mini tirade shaking his head in disgust.

Two of his colleagues smiled at each another and simultaneously said, "Value Protocol #1." The rest of the team smiled and nodded in agreement.

The executive grinned, thought for a few seconds, and said, "OK, how about this? I think we could fix this problem if we had a section on our internal website where all new information was posted in real time. People could check regularly and have access to the most current information."

The members of the group agreed, a change was ultimately made, and the problem no longer exists as a routine characteristic of their business culture. In this case, his suggestion was a good one and ultimately improved the business process.

It's important to note that this value protocol doesn't require someone's solution to be Nobel Prize–worthy. Doing this well does not require one to have the best solution. It is intended purely to optimize the way people think and problem-solve by requiring people to be constructive and not merely critical.

Another example was an employee who complained about holding too many staff meetings. There were those who grumbled and nodded in agreement, while others appeared indifferent and expressionless.

Almost as an afterthought, one of the participants declared that the group had just trampled upon this newly agreed value protocol of offering a recommendation with every criticism. He asked the colleague who raised the complaint what she thought might fix it.

After some back-and-forth discussion and input from many team members, a solution emerged to have staff meetings at different intervals. One regular meeting scheduled for the first Monday of every month with tentative weekly dates held on their calendars for the balance of the month. A notice would be sent out on the Friday prior to the meeting date to determine need. The manager would review team input and decide by mid-afternoon if there was sufficient need for a meeting on the upcoming Monday. As of this book's printing, the solution continues to work well for their team.

I don't want to be naïve or blind to the occasional need for unabashed venting. Sure, there are times when opening the sliding door, stepping out on the balcony, closing it firmly behind you, and yelling at the top of your lungs is an important, and even necessary, emotional release. However, those should be few and far between!

There are no doctors to prescribe a cure for business problems. Both the diagnoses and treatments must come from within. This value protocol provides the means to do just that.

2. START WITH "YES"

This value protocol goes to the epicenter of the human psyche. It is an axiom and maybe even too platitudinous to say that we all want to feel validated. There is a critical yet subtle difference between placation and validation. After one has offered an idea, there is that brief moment of anticipation, wondering how it will be received. "Will they like it, be indifferent to it, or simply hate it?" Clearly, we all would like our ideas to be thought of as brilliant and indispensable.

In any meeting or conversation where there are differences of opinion, those differences are often interpreted as being adversarial. There is almost an implied, silent no preceding a challenge to the statement.

Our instinct sometimes causes us to be defensive and push back.

To minimize the appearance of defensiveness, always provide a value comment about anything someone says or does. Begin your response with "Yes" and briefly acknowledge appreciation for the value of the person's remark.

Some might claim it's too difficult, or even pretentious, to tell someone that there is value in a statement, especially if you strongly disagree with their idea. It's not!

You can almost always find some value in any idea. Here's a fun example to illustrate how this can be accomplished.

Someone asked me to demonstrate how this could be done by presenting me with a very challenging scenario. I was asked how

I could possibly respond with a yes if the person's suggestion was, "People who have not earned a college degree should not be allowed to vote." Clearly, an absurd proposition!

> **There is a critical yet subtle difference between placation and validation.**

Here's one possible response, starting with "yes":

> "Yes, I can see how restricting voting to those with a higher level of education might suggest they are better informed. But what is the spirit and intent of the Constitution and is there any valid correlation between one's formal education and the selection of a candidate?"

The discussion can continue along many branches at this point, but there will undoubtedly be a higher level of respect and engagement by initially acknowledging and demonstrating your understanding of the other person's thoughts versus beginning your response with, "No, you're wrong."

This doesn't mean that each and every time someone makes a remark, we should start with the word "yes." You'll need to use your discretion to determine when and how frequently this approach should be applied. But "Yes, I understand," or "I see your point," followed with elaboration, will always relax the curtains of opposition and open the doors for productive discussion.

3. ALWAYS ASK MEETING ATTENDEES FOR INPUT AND PERSPECTIVE

No team or group meeting should conclude without every participant being expected to contribute. During the natural flow of discussion, addressing someone by name and simply asking for their opinion on the topic accomplishes a number of very positive outcomes.

First, new ideas and perspectives will be brought to the table. Also, people will see you as a leader who values the team's input. More importantly, it actually *makes* you a better leader and brings out the best from everyone with whom you work.

For this value protocol, timing is particularly important. I wouldn't advise starting off a discussion by turning to one of the meeting attendees and asking for the person's opinion. Allow the discussion to flow naturally, even if one or two people initially monopolize the discussion. After there has been some reasonable exchange, addressing someone by name who has not yet participated and simply inviting his or her opinion on the topic significantly raises the level of engagement from everyone.

4. ENSURE TIMELY DISTRIBUTION OF INFORMATION

Access to information is a cornerstone of success. When we obtain new information, whether through formal organizational channels or casual conversations, we use that knowledge to help improve our quality of work.

Consider all information that comes to your attention and assess whether it may have value for others in support of performance. If the answer is yes, this value protocol suggests that you share it and explain the reasons you've chosen to distribute it to others.

Unfortunately, we sometimes sit on that information and don't give careful thought to the value it may provide others. After all, the more information people have access to, the less likely they are to *make "stuff" up*!

There has been much talk about fake news and people operating on bad or unreliable information. When people have the most current, relevant, and accurate information, it fuels their ability to make better decisions. Do research, not me-search!

The evolved leader keeps a sharp eye out for any information encountered that may enable colleagues to perform their jobs more accurately and effectively. In addition to improving the work process, being vigilant in this effort sends a clear message to the recipients that you have a genuine interest in their success. This is a value protocol you should instill as common practice for all members of your team.

When there are gaps in facts, people make "stuff" up! Do research, not me-search!

---

5. ROUTINELY PROVIDE DEVELOPMENTAL FEEDBACK

Feedback too often carries an imbalanced tone of negative input versus constructive commentary. This may be a contributing factor to why feedback occurs less frequently than it should.

For decades, in jobs I held in the corporate world, I typically received feedback on a preset, scheduled cycle. That feedback came during either my annual performance review or a monthly progress report with my boss. Unfortunately, only receiving feedback at these intervals left wide gaps of time. Moreover, the feedback was more often of an assessment of what had been done versus providing proactive constructive development along the way.

Constructive feedback should be shared *regularly* and as close to the related event as possible. Rich developmental feedback should also include recognition, acknowledgment, ideas, and suggestions, along with asking if help is needed.

Here are some suggested strategies to incorporate into your regular feedback with team members that can enhance their receptivity in receiving it.

Consider starting your feedback using the following opening statement: "Let me offer you some suggestions that might help next time." This statement conveys a genuine desire to help in one's development. It avoids a sense of scolding or judgment and, instead, makes the recipient more receptive to what he or she is about to hear.

Compare this approach where instead the opening remark of the feedback may have been beginning your feedback with, "Let me tell you what you did wrong." That message is more likely to shut someone down. The recipient only needs to hear that one time, and it's likely they will not want to hear any more of your feedback.

Managers giving feedback using this blunt wording may, indeed, believe they have executed the process "correctly." There, task completed! In fact, there's nothing technically wrong with that opening. However, it seems indisputable that the approach where the manager "offers suggestions that might help" leaves the recipient infinitely more receptive and accepting of the balance of your feedback.

Consider asking what you can do to help in the process. Is there anything that the person may need, or is there something you can do specifically to help? Even when the answer is no, let them know that the door is open and they won't be negatively judged for asking.

6. START BROADLY

Many workplace problems don't get resolved, because we instinctively go directly to the symptom of the problem. Unfortunately, this can be as ineffective as treating a wound by wrapping it with duct tape. The bleeding stops, and the wound is no longer visible. Treating the symptom has never been the best way to cure the problem.

In the workplace, I recommend starting broad and funneling down to capture all the branches that contribute to the cause of the problem.

Here's a typical example. In addressing the issue of equal pay for women in the workplace, one Wall Street firm focused directly on the symptom and put a plan in place to raise the salaries of female workers to match that of their male counterparts. However, they failed to take into consideration the broader issues contributing to pay disparity, including tenure and performance history. Although one may have the same job title as another person, someone who has been in the assignment for 10 years might logically merit higher compensation than someone who just stepped into the position. And clearly, someone with a consistent history of top performance ratings would merit higher annual increases than someone with moderate ratings.

But this is a broader brush than something as single-dimensional as tenure. Other factors need to be considered in determining pay equity. These might include educational background, industry group affiliations, performance at other companies, and unique levels of expertise.

Evolved leaders assess the breadth and the farthest reach of a problem's tentacles, beyond what is immediately apparent. When making decisions, always ask for perspective on the underlying causes and influencing factors that have led to the problem, in advance of formulating a solution.

7. DON'T WAIT—INITIATE

Whenever there is an issue, be the one who takes the initiative to bring it to the table.

Disharmony, disagreement, and dissent abound in the normal course of business. More often than not, people tend to avoid conflict and confrontation. It's easier to say, "I love the emperor's new clothes" than to be the one to call out his full-frontal nudity.

Don't sit safely blending into the camouflage. Standing up to authority certainly has its risks and is likely the reason avoidance is often a preferred choice, but no one has ever achieved leadership greatness by going with the flow and becoming the lemming. You'll be safe but never admired.

As with most of our value protocols, there's an element of art to this process. Good judgment plays a key role in deciding when and how to initiate discussion. In some instances, avoidance may be the preferred act of wisdom. In other words, "Know when to fold 'em. Know when to walk away." There are, however, clever ideas and thoughts we have floating in the periphery of our minds that we allow to lie dormant. If these have potential value, bring them to the forefront and take the initiative to lay them out for the team to review.

Don't sit safely blending into the camouflage.

Here are some guidelines for orchestrating the "when" and "how" to initiate.

Start with identifying whether the issue is major or relatively benign. Never waste your time on those that are unimportant unless they are easy to capture as low-hanging fruit.

In other words, if calling out a problem is likely to gain group support, even if it isn't critical to the business, take advantage of that opportunity to establish yourself as a leader who recognizes when there is an opportunity for improvement and seizes it. If, on the other hand, calling out an issue will gain little benefit and also has a high probability of pushback, just let it go.

The evolved leader seeks truth over comfort.

When calling out an issue that has the potential of making notable change, anticipate the likely objections and risks, and prepare how you may best present it. This is the fundamental process of how a trial lawyer presents a case in the courtroom. No lawyer ever asks a question of a witness for which they don't already know the answer. If the witness deviates from that answer, the attorney is fully prepared to eviscerate the testimony and gain the support of the jury.

I'm not suggesting the hot, eviscerating style of the courtroom for your staff meetings, but it is a line of thinking that can prepare you for initiating constructive confrontation. Anticipate the likely objections, and prepare a convincing line of logic to support your position.

The evolved leader seeks truth over comfort. Ask yourself, Have I seen or heard something I disagree with that, if changed, would greatly benefit the business or group performance? If so, initiate the discussion.

In short, find what needs to be done to improve the business—and doing it will always be more admired than waiting to be told what to do.

8. LISTEN WITH THE INTENT OF UNDERSTANDING

Listening means hearing what others are saying and trying to understand its value.

The conventional interpretation of listening is limited to what we hear. In truth, the objective of listening is to focus on genuinely attempting to uncover the sender's central message.

This value protocol relates to the important distinction between denotation and connotation. As covered earlier, the more accurate and precise method to discern what a message is communicating is through its connotation, which often includes far more than the words themselves.

When there are differences of opinion, all too often, the listening filters are not well calibrated. When this occurs, we strategically listen for what we can use to counter the opposing view.

For some people, an opposing viewpoint becomes a challenge. They lie in wait, not listening for content but instead listening with two objectives: first, for weaknesses in what the other has said and second, for a break of silence to spring into action and counter.

Beware the person who pulls the critical thinking defense. Critical thinking is a good thing. It is the opposite of groupthink. Critical thinking finds the soft spots, weak links, and hidden landmines. This too is a good thing. Being good at critical thinking, however, isn't just about being critical. The more respected and admired leader is the one who assesses first for value before shining a laser on any areas that can be improved upon. Some of the "spring-to-criticize" behavior is rooted deep in the marrow of highly competitive people who have not developed the skill of balance. They have the social need to be the smartest person in the room (SIR) whenever a discussion is launched. This can be a dangerous arena in which to play when it's a common profile of the workplace culture you operate in. SIRs tend not to back down, even in the face of logic and reason. The best question to ask them is, "Did you see any value in what I said?" There is a better than even chance they will pause, reset, and acknowledge some level of value in one's contribution.

I routinely interact with someone who prides herself as a critical thinker. Her standard modus operandi is to politely listen to a business proposition and then launch into a comprehensive assessment of the problems she alone sees. The remarks are often void of any acknowledgment of value. The comments are not presented as suggestions or alternative viewpoints, but more the facts that need to be corrected. Her critical comments are often quite useful and do offer ways to improve the project but this is not critical thinking—it's just being critical. Her remarks often conclude with a silent but implied, "Case closed!"

Recipients of such single dimensional critical commentary can become defensive. They turn off their filters that, if done better, would allow them to hear the valuable constructive feedback.

Critical thinking is not about criticizing alone. It is the balanced process of sifting through the wheat and the chaff of what people offer and showing appreciation for what proves to provide value as well as what can be made better.

People see what they seek and hear what they expect. Set the sights for your team members to not just hear what colleagues are saying, but to *listen* for understanding and acknowledging value before criticizing.

9. VALIDATE—DON'T SPECULATE

You've certainly heard it before. Ask five people their interpretation of what was said, and you'll get five different answers. Unfortunately, we allow those different interpretations to remain ill-defined and unconfirmed.

This value protocol is quite straightforward. Never allow yourself to be in a position of acting upon something you heard, only to later discover that you had failed to validate and misinterpreted the original message.

In very crisp terms, this value protocol reminds you to never allow yourself to have a knee-jerk response before validating.

The receiver interprets the message and acts on it accordingly, based on their understanding. It is the responsibility of the receiver of the message to validate his or her interpretation before acting on it.

Don't act on speculation, assumptions, or unconfirmed beliefs. Actively seek clarification and validate before you act.

Evolved leaders develop the skill to assess the breadth of someone's proposal or suggestion and use connective language to share both the value they find, as well as where they feel it could be improved upon.

ACTIVE APPLICATION

It is your responsibility to establish a culture in which everyone understands what you expect in order to practice solution-based thinking. Ensure your team keeps this filter active and in the forefront of their practice.

Infusing these value protocols into a team's routine workplace interactions should be a defining characteristic of your leadership profile and business culture.

CHAPTER 10

Recruiting and Keeping Talented People

This chapter will examine new concepts and skills in the areas of talent identification, retention, and workplace skills development.

It is well established that relationships forged at an early age are often the most deeply rooted bonds we form as discussed in Chapter 3. There are powerful ways to apply this concept in sourcing and building talent within your teams that also have long-term impact.

In my community, four of the eight couples with whom we regularly socialize met their spouses while in college. Decades later, those relationships remain deeply intact. Early connections often foster long-term bonds and commitment.

Why is this cultural dynamic of early connections to build high-performance teams important?

Developing talent, of course, can only be achieved once people are on board. Identifying top talent, however, is a sifting process that continues to morph as business cultures and employee expectations evolve. The process begins with innovative sourcing methods to identify top talent capable of propelling a business forward in a rapidly changing marketplace. Achieving this requires a different set and higher degree of interviewing skills and techniques than utilized by many hiring managers today.

SOURCING TALENT

To broaden your opportunity to discover the gems, throw your net wide. Although prestigious schools are often targeted for recruitment, don't be fooled. Most Fortune 1000 CEOs and senior executives did not attend an Ivy League college or top university.

To illustrate the power that evolved leadership skills can have in the sourcing process, let's begin with the age-old college and university job fair sourcing approach. It's very much like a humpback whale's wide-mouth gulp—but instead of pulling in a pool of krill, the company pulls in a pool of candidates. Just like the whale filters out the krill from the detritus, the company filters out the best candidates from the also-rans. The problem is: Every company at job fairs uses the same basic filtering process and flags those high-potential candidates for follow-up.

Recruiting companies will sell candidates the same fundamental pitch about their company's products, services, prestige, compensation, and benefits. Of course, all of that is important—but the evolved leader talks about culture and even takes it to the next level, on-site, asking questions such as:

▶ "If you were to create your own company, what would be unique about its culture that would make it great?"

▶ "People tend to leave companies after about three or four years. What would a company be like for you to want to stay there longer?"

▶ "At our company, a cornerstone of our culture is that every employee, whether long term or a new hire, is given the opportunity to contribute ideas and perspectives on how to optimize the corporate culture and job experience. Is that something that would be important to you?"

Exploring these and other unique areas of interest will enhance the appeal of your company.

EARLY INTERNSHIPS AS COMPETITIVE ADVANTAGE

It won't take more than one summer of internship to identify whether the students you recruit are capable and can perform to the levels you set. For the ones that do, don't let them slide by. Indoctrinate them into the authentic workplace culture. Don't coddle them. Hold them accountable. Place the same level of expectation on them as you would any full-time new hire. Give them rich, developmental feedback. Nurture those that do well, and jettison those that don't measure up.

For most internship programs, the projects assigned are rife with low-level, dispassionate busywork, devoid of true workplace challenge. The assigned tasks tend to run only on the periphery of the core business. Interns often sit in the shadows. For many, it's not uncommon for their learning to be accomplished through osmosis. The evolved leader makes internship programs highly developmental and well structured.

Meet with interns weekly to provide assessment and developmental feedback. Most important, give them license to openly challenge ideas, and reward them when they do. Solicit their opinions about the job, the work, the team, the environment, their satisfaction level, and the workplace culture.

Rest assured, when a student has interned with a company that provides this level of engagement and development for three successful and enriching summers, that rich experience creates a magnetic attraction when the time comes to transition to full time employment.

Another tactic for the evolved leader's recruitment arsenal is to consider meeting with various department heads, such as business, technology, or other departments of a college or university in your region. Consider offering to be a guest speaker on the topic in which your company has industry expertise.

Make sure your keynote is not a blatant, unabashed, and self-aggrandizing advertisement for your company. Ensure your message supports the broader mission of the program curriculum and your industry. However, don't miss the opportunity to include the alluring and exciting dynamics of your company in describing and illustrating key points.

Include real-life workplace challenges from your company, and ask the students to analyze and develop solutions. Direct them to work in small teams, and have each group select a spokesperson who will report back the findings to the larger group. Though not foolproof, this becomes a natural vetting process.

More than likely, those who take on the spokesperson role are natural leaders and the candidates to focus on. Ask each of the spokespeople to write down their group's findings and bring them to you at the close of the session. Get those students' contact information, give them yours, encourage them to reach out for more information about your company, and suggest they consider an internship.

If you're thinking this might be a promising approach but should be passed along to someone in HR to do, you would be "unevolvedly" mistaken. Unless, of course, the position in question is in HR. Otherwise, candidates are more inspired when they speak directly to managers or people doing the specific work in which they are interested.

Although companies source candidates through multiple channels, the overwhelming favorites are web-based services. Not only do these provide the largest volume of candidates; they also provide excellent honing and vetting tools that accelerate the search process. But while these are well established and popular, we will not spend time focusing on this option.

The exponential advancement of AI vetting algorithms significantly enhance and accelerate the filtering process. However, employee referrals add what might be considered a personal link. Employee referrals tend to be exceptionally effective, as no one knows your company and its culture demands better than those already immersed within it.

An employee, once hired, is more likely to focus on doing a good job when a friend's or a family member's reputation is on the line for having recommended that person to the organization.

People who currently work for you understand the dynamics, performance expectations, work relationships, culture, workload, required skills and, in general, "the way things are done here." If you refer a candidate and they get hired and excel, it reflects positively on you. Conversely, if the person crashes and burns, it runs the risk of damaging your reputation. For this reason, push employee referrals higher on your list as a prioritized recruitment tool.

Communicate to all your staff the value and importance of their referrals to building the organization. Encourage them to recommend qualified friends and acquaintances.

In a conversation with HR executives at a technology company, they shared that over 70 percent of their new hires came through this powerful channel. Many companies recognize its value and pay employees a generous finder's fee if their referral is hired. The fee is usually paid only after the new hire has completed the standard probationary period, typically 90 days.

HOW TO INTERVIEW AND EVALUATE CANDIDATES

Let's examine the interview process itself.

Whether the interview is conducted via a virtual platform or in-room face-to-face, when interviewing a candidate, the obvious first step is to assess the technical skills and knowledge required to perform the job. Of course, that aspect is a given. Once a candidate's technical qualifications have been established, the evolved leader looks at the equally important high-functioning skills for success. Each of these fall within the realm of business intelligence, such an immensely broad topic that we certainly can't cover its magnitude here. But let's examine four cornerstones.

- ▶ Communication
- ▶ Agility/catching the curveball
- ▶ Creativity
- ▶ Taking initiative

Communication

While technical skills are the metaphorical "dress code" for entry into the halls of leadership, effective communication is the "cover charge." One's ability to understand, reason, analyze, draw inference, and effectively communicate a concept, is a powerful asset.

Historically, businesses have valued formal education as a measure of one's intelligence. In recent years, some companies have dropped the requirement of a college degree as a prerequisite altogether and view a college education as less important than the candidate's ability to think, reason, and communicate well.

Meet with the key stakeholders in your company. Take the evolutionary step to discuss whether that traditional requirement should continue to be a prerequisite for identifying top talent. You may find value in pushing the college degree requirement off the list.

Having punched a ticket at a university provides evidence of one's discipline, particularly in the area of memorizing facts, drawing inferences, and meeting requirements. These may also be valuable skills in the workplace but are not necessarily the dominant skills needed to perform well on a project team, or as a team or group leader within an organization.

When technical skills are similar across various candidates, don't hesitate to hire the one demonstrates the ability to present an idea in a compelling way enabling everyone on the team to understand the proposed benefits.

Communicating one's outbound messages is just one direction. The other, of course, is having the ability for interpreting inbound messages as well. This includes the higher aptitude and agility for catching the unpredictable curve balls of business, over those candidates who merely performed well on their college exams.

Agility/Catching the Curveball

Within this high-functioning skill of intelligence is the particularly unique quality of being able to catch the curveball—a metaphor for the candidate's agility to grasp and manage the unpredictable and demonstrate the ability to craft immediate solutions. Many leaders have found themselves short-circuited when hit by a lightning strike of unanticipated events or situations.

One clever and very effective technique that tests a candidate's ability to do this I learned from Ritch Gaiti, a former senior IT director at Bank of America. This strategy reaches far beyond conventional approaches and clearly reveals one's ability to catch and field the proverbial curveball. Here's how it works.

When interviewing a candidate, after your initial greeting and pleasantries, state the following: "I'm sure you've given some careful thought in preparing for our meeting today. There are, no doubt, questions you've anticipated I would ask and you've prepared for these. I'd like to turn the interview over to you. Please tell me everything you feel I should learn about you and what makes you an excellent candidate for this position. So let me hand the interview over to you."

After handing the reins over to the candidate, the first five seconds will reveal significant information about the person's ability and agility to handle an uncomfortable and even awkward curveball. The response will range from the proverbial "deer in the headlights" (in this case, high-beam halogens) to composure and control, where the person takes a few moments, collects their thoughts, organizes what to say, and jumps right in.

You're looking for someone who can perform well and comfortably respond to the uncomfortable.

Here's what to look for. Do they demonstrate in their initial remarks an understanding of the position, the technical qualifications required, and their proven skills to meet or exceed those requirements? If their description indicates a misunderstanding of the position or the qualifications needed, you should jump in at this early stage and provide some clarification. Otherwise, their response should reflect how their current responsibilities and proven skills match with the job qualifications for the position. Your top candidates will likely include commentary about the company and various aspects of why they would want to work within your culture.

Be prepared. Many candidates are thrown by this unexpected challenge. Don't cast them off if they seem befuddled. Provide some basic guidance on the categories you would like them to cover. You're not looking for someone to purely execute tasks; you're looking for someone who can perform well and who comfortably respond to the uncomfortable.

Another clear skill that reveals itself in this process is the person's mental organizational thinking skills. When done well, the order would be defining the job, listing the skills required, matching his or her skills with those requirements, providing examples that demonstrate or confirm those skills, and describing how he or she successfully delivered upon those in the past.

For the candidate that aces this interview structure, you have likely uncovered a multicarat diamond in the rough.

The skill of catching the curveball and fielding it well should not be limited to sourcing new candidates. As the evolved leader, continuing to develop the agility of your employees internally is a key ingredient to building high-performance teams.

In a conversation with Mark Pearson, CEO of Equitable, the high-functioning skill of agility consumed a major part of our conversation. He shared some of his thoughts on its value: "The need for agility is essential, as a leader, to be able to adapt to circumstances you encounter. You must have the agility to adapt to the environment. Sometimes leaders find themselves in a particular role of command and control like before an orchestra; while at other times, there's a need to allow the individual musicians the flexibility to be creative and collaborate in the composition of something new through the power of their combined skills. This ability to show agility to change with the circumstances is a skill I value and look for."

Mark Pearson's comment about the importance of agility was echoed by senior leaders in a variety of industries during interviews conducted for this book. Notably, it holds true for even small, regional, and local businesses, as well.

> The need for agility is essential, as a leader,
> to be able to adapt to circumstances you encounter.
> This ability to show agility to change with the
> circumstances is a skill I value and look for.
> —Mark Pearson, CEO, Equitable

Creativity

Another aspect of business intelligence is creativity, a difficult skill to quantify. The term "creativity" is often interchanged with "innovation"—though not synonyms, they are intertwined. Creativity pertains to thoughts, ideas, and concepts. Innovation is about putting those thoughts and ideas into action and making them tangible.

The symbiotic relationship between these two terms is that they are sequential. One cannot apply a new concept until his or her creative skills have conceived it. The significance of balancing these two functions is that one can have the most forward-thinking vision and cerebrally profound thoughts and concepts, but they remain functionally worthless if not transformed and put into action. These two skills represent both sides of the futuristic coin. Sadly, there are far more great creative ideas than there are innovative plans to put them into action and effect meaningful change.

If someone were asked just a couple decades ago what they would want their phone to be able to do, it's unlikely the response would rattle off a list of features that today are staples of our handheld devices.

I can't quite imagine someone looking at a hardwired wall phone with its coiled cord, microphone, and receiver and spout a wish list that included making the unit wireless, infinitely portable, and able to operate in any mode of transport; providing the capability to stream movies; serving as a primary video and still camera; and an endless list of apps and features that are now standard offerings.

Of course, back then, there must have been many creative minds who did, in fact, envision these futuristic concepts. It took innovators to harness that creativity and make it a reality.

This is not to suggest that everyone seeking to be an evolved leader needs to change the fundamentals of human life in such profound ways, but in order to truly achieve greatness in your arena, it is necessary to shift one's thinking to uncover the power of what is not immediately apparent or common practice today.

Creativity and innovation are some of the most valued skills in any forward-thinking organization. Asking challenging, open-ended questions that fall outside the mainstream is one way to uncover these talents when interviewing candidates.

Here is another open-ended question you might pose to a candidate to reveal this talent: "What do you think our industry is not providing today that it should provide in the future?"

Hold onto the person who tells you something you haven't heard before.

People often wonder whether creativity is a natural skill or one that can be trained and developed. The answer is yes to both. There are some who display creativity as early as toddlers, but the skill can be learned and developed. I say this with the same degree of certainty as knowing that the technology I'm using today will be a near Jurassic artifact in the next decade.

Techniques for building a team's creative thinking skills will be explored in more detail in Chapter 11.

Taking Initiative

Early in my career, I was given great advice from Ritch Gaiti, whom I mentioned earlier in the chapter. He took me on a brief tour of the highlights of his career. I learned that four of his last seven jobs had not existed until he created them. I was a bit puzzled and didn't fully grasp the value of this message until he outlined it.

He went on to say that 50 percent of the jobs that exist today did not exist 10 years earlier. He predicted this pattern would continue over the next 10 years, as well. Ritch was only slightly off with that prediction. In fact, it's been closer to 70 percent.

His strategy was artful. He would scan the current landscape of his functional area and industry. Next, he would analyze industry news and financial trends to glean their future impact on his company. He would approach his bosses and outline the importance of staying a step ahead of the curve and offer to take on the newly identified area and fold it into the sphere of his current job responsibilities. He would make a strong case and his leaders bought into his vision.

As his predictions panned out and affirmed his insight, vision, and value to the company, his roles expanded exponentially. In some cases, the growth spawned a fully independent new business area. His words still resonate with me: "Don't go for the job that exists. Create the *new* job and lead it."

In your search for candidates, look for those who in their own way demonstrate the capacity for taking initiative. You might ask this question directly: "You've demonstrated how you were able to complete your assigned tasks well. Can you give me an example of what no one asked you to do, where you took the initiative, identified it, and got it done?"

> **Don't go for the job that exists.**
> **Create the *new* job and lead it.**
> —Ritch Gaiti, former senior IT director, Bank of America

You should be looking for people who don't just follow directions, but have the ability to independently identify what needs to get done and take the initiative to do it.

STAY INTERVIEWS

Everyone has heard of exit interviews. These are the final meetings with employees after they've resigned from a company. Resignations often come as a surprise to bosses who find themselves after the exit interview in a state of lamentation, humming the lyrical refrain, "You don't know what you've got till it's gone."

Whether the person resigning is a highly desired top performer or just a near invisible cog in the business engine, when the person has announced the intent to leave, the knee-jerk reaction of most bosses is to wonder why—and that question usually is the underlying driver in conducting the exit interview.

Resignations also conjure up questions of risk. Did we screw up and are we a valuable resource to the competition? Even if the person is an average performer, we still want to know why the employee is breaking up with us.

When the resigning employee is a top performer, it reverberates more deeply within the business psyche, pinches a sensitive nerve, and triggers an all-out courting to woo the person back and dissuade the departure. To keep valued employees, I've heard everything from offering to match and even exceed the other offer by a sizable percentage, to offering a promotion, to even offering an off-cycle bonus grant. In most cases, these flattering counteroffers end up being too little, too late.

A QUICK SIDE NOTE: COUNTEROFFERS OFTEN BACKFIRE

Sometimes an employee is so impressed with the company's generous counteroffer and effort to keep them, the person will accept the counteroffer and stay. The company feels successful in convincing the employee to remain, but this is often a short-lived glory, as buyer's remorse tends to creep in as the employee's underlying "disloyalty" rises to the forefront.

I have never seen anyone who accepted a counteroffer later rise to new heights within the organization. People question the genuineness of the employee's commitment and question whether that person will again (in nonlegal terms) be a flight risk. After all, the person has telegraphed that he or she is only in it for the money.

This is reminiscent of the routine behavior from my dog Milo. If I toss him a potato chip, he'll sniff it, turn up his nose, and walk away. But if I reach for it, he'll lunge at light speed and gobble it down, demonstrating what I call "I only want it when I know someone else wants it" syndrome.

Exit interviews are right out of the playbook. Sometimes companies act like Milo. A company will lunge to get that employee back, simply because someone else wants them. And as with Milo, the decision doesn't always settle well in the gut over time.

Companies profess to glean critical information from exit interviews to better understand the shortcomings and gaps that can be filled to discourage future losses—except for the people they want to jettison. In reality, it basically boils down to a data collection exercise and a "CYA" moment to cover up the legitimate reasons that someone chooses to resign.

How foolish to wait until someone is walking out the door to try and pull them back in. This is what the Stay Interview is designed to avert—the remorse everyone feels at the loss of a valued employee.

Why Do People Leave?

The pandemic of 2020 had a transformational impact on the ways people viewed the value of their work, the workplace, the balance of personal interests, and more. Many chose to leave the workplace entirely, a trend that came to be known by many names: the Great Resignation, powering down, quiet quitting, the Great Exodus, and so on.. This cultural transformation may well be the greatest shift to the structure of the traditional workplace.

The Millennials, Gen Xers, and Gen Zers of today's workforce are leaving their jobs with greater frequency and within shorter periods of employment than in the past. Regardless to one's generational affiliation, it is well established that pay is not the primary reason people leave their jobs.

"More employees are voluntarily leaving their jobs than at almost any other time," according to the *Harvard Business Review*.[1] Exit interviews indicate that culture has risen high on the list of motivating factors causing employees to stay or jump ship.

This is further reinforced by the study highlighted in Chapter 3, which highlighted that the number one reason people now leave job is toxic work culture. How do we mitigate this?

Mitigating a Toxic Culture

In the past decade, people have been focusing more and more on their quality of life, with the many hours they spend at work, whether in the office or remotely, factoring into that.

As an evolved leader, it is your role to fuel the talents and skills of your team.

You must strive to not only extinguish that toxicity in the work culture but create an environment that reaches beyond the fundamental matching of job skills and tasks. What is a toxic work environment? Employees define a toxic work environment as:

- ▶ Failure to promote inclusion
- ▶ Workers feeling disrespected
- ▶ Unethical behavior or low integrity
- ▶ Abusive management
- ▶ A cutthroat environment where colleagues feel they are actively undermined

Stay interviews are designed to uncover whether and the degree to which these sentiments are being felt by employees in your corporate culture. Stay interviews stem employee discontent and extinguish the desire to look outside your workplace for a culture fit.

Most notably, stay interviews are not a onetime event. For these to be effective, they should occur at least once or twice a year, possibly more frequently when symptoms of discontent are apparent.

It's your job, as the evolved leader, to constantly monitor the dashboard of your team to see if any "check engine" lights of discontent are flashing.

This approach prevents falling into the abyss of the "too little, too late" syndrome by pulsing the state-of-mind of employees. Stay interviews help managers understand what motivates employees to stay so that those factors can be reinforced. Most importantly, stay interviews can signal frustrations that can be averted early on.

Some companies believe they can identify these potentially toxic conditions through employee engagement surveys. It is true that this assessment tool reveals sentiments based on responses to key questions. But the reality is that checking a series of boxes is too broad-brushed and impersonal.

Imagine your life partner approaches you with survey questions to pulse the strength of your relationship. Your partner asks you to fill in the boxes on a scale of 1 to 5 about various aspects of the quality of your relationship.

Some glaring red flags might be called out, but unless you delve more deeply into the reasons for a low rating and what specifically can be done to remedy the condition, little, if any, change in sentiment occurs. Marriage counseling is a hybrid of exit interviews and stay interviews, with a statistically heavy leaning toward the exit side of the equation.

It's your job, as the evolved leader, to constantly monitor the dashboard of your team to see if any "check engine" lights of discontent are flashing.

STAY INTERVIEW SKILLS

Let's explore some of the key components of the stay interview.

The personal scale of commitment and connection for everyone is influenced by how much you are valued and appreciated by others. The failure that sometimes occurs is that people are not told this directly. My boss might believe that my value is made evident by the rating I receive on a performance review. No doubt, that carries importance. It doesn't, however, make me special. My father had 11 siblings. I can't imagine how difficult it would be to be an attentive, engaged parent with a dozen children. But he felt his mother did a good job by letting all members of their mini tribe know that she loved them. But he confided in me that he never really felt special.

All 12 children got what amounted to a delivered script of proper parental messages, but there was too much going on to zero in on the uniqueness of the individual. Being told you are good is never enough if what you need is to be made to feel special.

Here are the four basic steps to the stay interview process.

Step 1. Opening Comment

Start by telling the employee that you really appreciate having them on the team and that their contributions are an important part of why the team succeeds. Outline the details of what you appreciate most about them and that the company is very fortunate to have them be a part of the organization.

Step 2. Ask the Following Key Questions

- ▶ "How would you assess your level of contentment with your job and with the company?"
- ▶ "If you could change anything about the work you are assigned, what would it be?"
- ▶ "Are there any additional areas of responsibility you'd be interested in taking on?"
- ▶ "Is there anything about the company that makes you proud to be a part of what we stand for?"
- ▶ "Is there any area within the business that you are curious about and would like to learn more?"

Step 3. Work/Life Assessment

Ask, "Are there any personal situations outside the workplace that the company might be able to assist you with?"

Step 4. Close the Stay Interview

Ask, "Is there anything we haven't discussed that I can do to make your experience here better?"

The stay interview should last no more than 30 minutes. Your primary objective is to uncover specific frustrations or concerns about the job itself, the business culture, or the quality of your relationship with the employee in time to take action before it reaches the tipping point.

Addressing the Issues

The stay interview itself is relatively easy. The difficulty comes with addressing the issues that are uncovered. The ones you find easy to mitigate—do them! Others may require support from other people in the company. Begin that process without delay. Of course, some might not be doable or reasonable, at all. These might include requesting an exorbitant pay increase or other requests that fall outside the realm of what the business is able to provide.

In some cases, requests that might seem beyond reason should be considered. Even if you are not able to fully accommodate the request, you may be able to offer an alternative that sends a clear message that you have the person's best interests in mind.

Even when the employee does not request it, providing access to senior leaders, offering a title change, or involving the employee in special projects that provide visibility should be considered.

Sometimes a stay interview can uncover ways to retain employees on a broad scale. While in a regular business meeting at a large financial institution with my boss, it seemed clear he was distracted about something. He had read a report on company demographics and was disappointed with a continuing downward trend and expressed his concern about the stark disparities of gender and race at the top three senior levels, particularly SVPs and managing directors. There seemed to be a revolving door where hard work to bring people in appeared successful, when in fact equal numbers were exiting at the same time.

He said, "This is the literal example of taking two steps forward and three steps back."

In a tone of desperation, he looked squarely in my eyes and asked, "You've been at that level for several years now. Why are you still here?"

I cautiously pointed out the two possible interpretations of his question. First, was he trying to ascertain what the company could do that would encourage people at this level to stay? Or was he implying, "Why the hell are you still here?" The brief laugh eased the tension, and without hesitation, I told him, "I stay here because when

I'm at work I'm made to feel like I'm a part of the family. The moment I start feeling that I am merely a visitor, there's a good chance I would immediately start looking for another workplace family."

No one was able to categorize that the messages I had been receiving during my tenure were Tier #3 connective language interactions. Each day became a type of stay interview.

People will endure all sorts of workplace hardships, uncomfortable conditions, and other environmental challenges if they are made to feel valued, respected, and appreciated and enjoy the work they do. Your job as an evolved leader is to create that environment by uncovering the obstacles that might otherwise stand in the way.

CHAPTER 11

Axiological Skills for Evolved Leadership

Axiology is the philosophical study of value. The foundational messages in this book rest largely on creating messages of value that enable people to perform to their potential. The skills featured here represent nine key competencies necessary for effective leadership that infuse values into our evolved leadership aptitude.

For countless decades, published works on leadership have espoused the obvious and most fundamental skills to achieve leadership proficiency. For the most part, they have been—predictable, proverbial platitudes.

Becoming an evolved leader involves building a new set of philosophies and shaping the right set of behaviors to support them. Many of the core skills that pertain to successful leadership today have been with us a long time and will not go away. We will take a fresh look at some of those old standards and build upon them introducing a new, set of skills that support the demands and values of leadership's next generation by exploring a broad range of tactics, concepts, and techniques for optimizing leadership outcomes.

TOP LEADERSHIP SKILLS THROUGH A NEW LENS

In Chapter 1, we highlighted the core traits that define "leadership." Let's build on that further to shape its clarity and usability.

When I ask audiences to list the top traits of great leadership, those shown in Table 11.1 rise to the top, in no particular order. Throughout this chapter, we will merge the traditional definitions of leadership skills with a new expanded perspective for each trait to meet the demands of evolved leadership.

Respect	Effective communication	Persuasiveness
Intelligence	Active listening	Creativity and innovation
Integrity	Charisma	Sense of humor

TABLE 11.1   Classic Leadership Traits

RESPECT—AND BEING RESPECTED

Respect—and being respected—are the scaffolding upon which you enable the performance and skills of others.

Without respecting and being respected, people execute tasks through obligation, but not genuineness of purpose.

High-performance teams of the future must demand a culture that exudes these qualities. You will never be viewed as an admired leader who commands loyalty and commitment if those around you do not respect you as an individual.

Managers can misinterpret perceived respect and admiration when it is an act of obligatory cover-up and protection. Who isn't pleased with agreement of an idea from others? This is sometimes the result of "yes-people" wanting to butter up the boss. Sadly, it's hard to distinguish one from the other. Are they going along with your idea begrudgingly or out of a sense of admiration and respect. People will often do what they are told out of fear or obligation. But they will never truly be committed and respect you if they are not feeling respected, themselves.

Do not confuse respect with someone being nice, kind, or anything that could be misconstrued as a form of cajoling or pandering. At its foundation, respect is about equity, not equality. Let's take a look at a seemingly controversial new dimension of respect and draw a clear distinction between "respect" and "respectful."

I'm often asked, "Why should I have to fake respecting someone when I flat-out feel they don't deserve my respect?" Telling people to respect their colleagues is a DEI standard message. Unfortunately, it's one that can give DEI a bad rap. When a person feels that they're being told how to feel about someone, there is both emotional and intellectual pushback. Whether spoken directly or not, it suggests that we should put on a front. But everyone knows you can't legislate emotion. I can't tell you to like someone or think something is funny, so how then can we expect people to buy into accepting the directive to have respect for another?

The clear answer is, you can't and shouldn't! I don't want you to respect people. I want you to treat them *respectfully*. To respect people means they have earned your admiration because of specific actions that have led you to placing them in that position of esteem. In short, the aphorism "Respect is earned" is a truism I fully advocate.

For example, I don't respect people who gossip but would unquestionably treat them respectfully in the workplace. This means that they receive no different treatment in the ways I listen to their commentary, allocate appropriate time, consider their ideas and suggestions, and all other behavioral aspects of respectful inclusion in the workplace.

The ultimate example in illustrating this distinction is the behavior expected from a judge or law enforcement officer. Regardless of whether a judge respects the defendant, that judge has a responsibility to treat that defendant respectfully.

Your objective as an evolved leader is to focus your attention entirely on equitable treatment respectfully, regardless of your personal feelings about them.

At its foundation, respect is about equity, not equality.

Many leaders have proudly expressed that they treat people on their teams equally, sometimes extolling the sentiment, "I treat everyone the same." What a misguided approach, and it is certainly not the best way to demonstrate respect as an evolved leader.

Being treated respectfully doesn't mean equality or sameness. Parents should not treat their children the same. Each child has unique needs and talents. Both the evolved parent and the evolved leader should recognize this and modify the ways they provide development and guidance with one's unique learning-style differences in mind. The one action that remains the same is that each child or each colleague in the workplace is treated with equity.

At its foundation, respect is about equity, not equality.

Specifically, that means not exhibiting disproportionate treatment that puts someone down without having explicable due cause. And it means acknowledging everyone's presence, being open to their opinions, and responding with language that is not condescending, insulting, or indifferent.

For example, I have a son and a daughter. When they were young, I might come home from work and wrestle with my son. We'd find ourselves tumbling and jabbing each other playfully, but it was clear my daughter had no such interest. Conversely, there were other activities I did with her in which my son had no interest. Although our interactions were different, they both received and fully understood they were being treated with equitable levels of engagement, value, and love.

I'm often asked, "Does this mean I have to be a fake? What if I genuinely don't like someone? Are you telling me I have to send them messages of respect that don't represent my honest feelings?"

Let me be emphatically clear. No one should do anything under pretense or duress. You should, however, have the internal desire to be an effective, motivational, and inspirational leader who enables all people with whom you work to perform to their potential.

I can't overstate the importance of this distinction for parsing our honest feelings about someone from how we should treat people equitably.

Imagine having a conference with your child's teacher. During that discussion, you explain that your daughter feels the teacher doesn't like her. She thinks other students in the class are liked and respected but feels as if she is an outsider. You explain that your daughter can't put her finger on anything specific that was blatantly wrong, but clearly feels a difference in the way she is being treated, compared with other classmates.

Would it be acceptable for the teacher to respond, saying, "Your daughter probably feels that way because I just don't like her," followed by, "Shouldn't I be honest and not fake it?" In what world would that be an acceptable response?!

Educators, at all levels, have a responsibility to ensure that all students are treated respectfully, are encouraged, and given equitable opportunities to live up to their potential. Even if a student is a poor performer, an educator must always deliver messages of equity to fuel the child's drive for success.

Great leaders are driven by the desire to enable all the members on a team and all with whom they work to perform to their potential. If done under duress, one should reevaluate whether leadership is the right role for them.

The key message here is that you cannot be an evolved leader if you are not able to send respectful, equitable messages that support a culture that enables everyone to perform to their fullest potential.

INTELLIGENCE

Intelligence reigns supreme as a top leadership skill and will likely hold that prestigious position until its predicted successor, AI, potentially eliminates the need for leaders as we know it. Intelligence has always been a cornerstone of success for any business mission. It is one of the sparks that ignites a team's raw skills, combining the natural glitter of innate skills with the highly polished facets of learned skills, otherwise known as "nature versus nurture." When we explored intelligence earlier, we noted that it is one of the top high-functioning skills and initially defined as being agile (able to hit curveballs) and highly creative.

Building on this definition, intelligence also requires the need to be well informed and the ability to decipher and translate both the complex and simple to levels that others may not see. Most importantly, intelligence means using information to become more effective and not merely to foresee what is needed today, but to anticipate future trends, demands, requirements, and market direction and shape a vision.

In the leadership arena, intelligence also defines one's ability to perceive detailed information and not miss the finer points—and then to have the agility to draw inferences and connect ideas in new ways that may otherwise be missed. The evolved leader never approaches an issue with an intractable position of certainty.

Evolved leaders draw out the perspective of team members and teach them to manage the web of resolution, a technique that draws out the many perspectives, isolates those viewpoints with clarity, and links their common threads. When the web is pulled, those ideas that have the strongest connections become the most firmly held and viable.

The evolved leader never approaches an issue with an intractable position of certainty.

In some instances, this process happens organically. Evolved leaders actively take it from random to a well-orchestrated and mechanized process. Perceptive leaders come to learn the profiles, styles, and strengths of all the members of their team. This process reaches beyond merely tapping into the strengths and developing the weaknesses of individuals. It endeavors to forge what I call a "collegial immersion bond" (CIB), a style of workplace pairing in the spirit of opposites attract. In this case, the theory is that opposites invigorate thinking and develop one another.

I watched this process emerge with several team members in a marketing organization. The leader paired one team member, who had impeccable organizational skills, with another team member, who was weak in this area but had unusually strong creative thinking skills. Rather than simply exposing them to one another, the leader gave explicit development direction to focus on skills transfer.

The highly organized employee did not just do his thing. An added responsibility was a training component to identify organizational lapses and to provide support to his CIB partner who was building skills in his respective area. Of course, the river flowed in both directions. When the highly organized CIB partner became too mechanical in the process, the creative partner would provide mutual developmental insight. It became quite noticeable that each had developed exponentially through the shared strength of the CIB partnership.

The benefits of this approach reach far beyond merely developing and expanding one's skill set. The broader benefit comes with creating an environment and culture that is magnetic. People experience work in ways that they otherwise would not. The bonds that are built across team members reflect a growth in mutual respect and a sense of value. It is a near utopian experience to know that you have had an impact on the development of your colleagues and that your difference is *valued* as part of what makes that business a success.

Instead of allowing this to randomly occur, the evolved leader cultivates this process.

The dynamics of most work teams encompass a range of personality types. There are extroverts, whose opinions are easily gleaned, while more reticent personalities may hesitate to offer their insights. There is no direct correlation between levels of verbal participation, intelligence, and the quality of workplace perspectives and ideas.

For the evolved leader, intelligence is manifested by never relying on dominant personalities to rule group thinking. It is essential to develop the skill to read the micromessages of team members that reveal disagreement, confusion, resistance, or support.

A raise of the eyebrow, a look of dismay, a tilt of the head that might imply a "so-what" reaction, should spark a clarion call to zero in on those subtle messages to decipher their underlying meaning. After observing someone's micromessage of objection, one could easily say, "That head tilt is telling me you're not in full agreement with what Joseph just said. I'd like to hear your perspective."

I'm sure there are many of you thinking, "Of course, I always ask people for their opinions in meetings."

The reality is, those broad-brush conventional statements such as, "Tell me what you think," tend to lead to nonconfrontational, safe responses. When you identify a specific behavior or a "tell," consider calling your observation out directly. I have often found that by simply stating the action you observed that indicated disagreement and then ending your remarks with, "Did I misread that?," they are more likely to feel more comfortable in expressing an honest opinion.

Whether one is charismatic or reserved, a balance must be struck across team members to draw out innovative solutions that otherwise may be missed. Diversity of thought is a powerful tool that stimulates innovative thinking of highly productive teams.

Intelligence also incorporates active research for staying current. You want to be the one who is seen as bringing the latest discoveries, innovative thinking, new trends, and most current research to the broader group. To do this, you have to read and uncover this information. By doing so, you will establish yourself as being inextricably linked with subject-matter intelligence.

A subset of intelligence is savviness, which is more closely related to emotional intelligence. Savviness takes a step beyond and incorporates the skill of being shrewd and able to read between the lines—and never be naïve about others who may try to take advantage of you or your team.

INTEGRITY

In the context of evolved leadership, integrity encompasses truthfulness and honesty. I recall sitting in a meeting with one of my tech clients in Silicon Valley. While reviewing our proposal for a new competency model, it became clear that one member of the team was not held in the same high regard as others.

At one point, that team member offered an observation about one detail we were discussing. Some members of the team looked at each other with an air of disdain and had an almost jocular and even dismissive response. Admittedly, the comment didn't show any deep insight or understanding, but the team leader did not fall victim to supporting the negative behavior.

Instead, she called it out, saying, "I don't understand your response. I'd like all of us to listen carefully to Jim's comment. If you disagree, please tell him so, and why." It was unquestionably clear that the manager assumed a near parental role, softly chastising the dismissive behavior of the team.

Far more important than the value of Jim's comment was the importance of making it clear that *all* opinions will be listened to, evaluated for their merit, and never dismissed based on who is saying it. No doubt, every team member walked away from that meeting with a higher regard for the integrity of the team leader and the value protocols of the team.

This is not to say that people should be coddled when they have bad ideas. It must be made clear that in no way should this approach be misinterpreted as indulging team members in poor thinking.

Predictive Behavior

The key message here is never letting filters of preconception of an individual be the reason for drawing conclusions. In other words, don't fall into the rut of predictive behavior. Don't assume that any idea coming from someone with a reputation for bad ideas *will* be an accurate predictor. Las Vegas has built a powerful industry off people who rely on their skills of prediction based on their interpretation of past activity.

The corollary is true, as well. Don't allow the halo effect to make a bad idea seem good.

I personally conducted an experiment in Boston that has been done in many academic settings around the world, with a professor at a liberal arts college. The professor created a file that contained 32 numbers. Upon completion of a writing assignment, students were instructed to access the file and select one of the 32 numbers, after which that number would be blocked to any other student, and use that number in place of their name in submitting their work. For this experiment, students were asked to submit their papers in printed form to maintain anonymity.

Once the papers were graded, the professor asked the students to provide their selected number and name. In speaking with him, he revealed there were three clear surprises. For the most part, students matched his predicted expectations of the grade received. In one case, though, the paper was given a C where the recipient turned out to be one of his best students, who typically received "A"s. His next comment revealed the power of this small blind experiment. He said, "Maybe I should reread that paper because I must have missed something."

There were two examples, however, where the reverse was true. High grades had been given to students he viewed as substandard performers. Not surprisingly, again he wanted to reread those papers once their identities had been revealed.

In this informal experiment, about 10 percent of his assumptions regarding his students' aptitudes proved to be flawed.

These types of assumptions reveal our predictive behavior in the workplace, as well. The source of the idea can lead us to biased interpretations of value. Great leaders should not lead with predictive behavior.

In the legal lexicon, there is the term "anticipatory breach." Normally, someone can only be sued for their failure to perform to the specifications of a contract only after the timeframes have expired. In other words, I can't sue a contractor for failing to complete the remodeling of my kitchen if the terms of the contract were to have the job completed in 90 days, until the 90 days have lapsed. But under certain circumstances, the law allows for a suit to be brought when there is a reasonable assumption that the contracted party will fail to fulfill the duties of the contracted work within the specified time frame.

If a contractor undertakes the job to demolish a structure and build a new two-car garage, a job that would normally take 6 to 8 weeks, and hasn't even begun demolition 5 weeks before the completion date, the court would allow legal proceedings to begin even before the official failed-to-complete date in the contract had passed.

Anticipatory breach may be valid in a courtroom, but not in our judgment of people in the workplace. As the evolved leader, you have a stake on both sides of the contract. You are responsible for assigning work to your team, but you must also take a role in supporting those who have been tasked with completing it, void of any predictive behavior.

EFFECTIVE COMMUNICATION

Although virtually everything in the world changes over time, one inextricable pairing is the interdependency of effective communication with great leadership. In Chapter 4 on connective communication, we examined the fundamental technical model of communication—sender, receiver, observer, and the critical responsibilities for these roles. Let's now explore some additional facets of this essential leadership jewel.

Although virtually everything in the world changes over time, one inextricable pairing is the interdependency of effective communication with great leadership.

Effective communication must be mastered across four dimensions:

- ▶ Clear and accurate message transfer
- ▶ Active listening
- ▶ Personal carriage
- ▶ Charisma

Clear and Accurate Message Transfer

It's well understood that clear, concise message transfer is a key leadership requirement. Our focus is not on the fundamental, remedial skills of communication. Let's take a step through the evolved leader portal.

In written communication, the process of honing multiple drafts to shape tone and clarity of a message is the routine. People will spend an inordinate amount of time writing just a few paragraphs of a business proposal, report, or communication. The first pass typically sets the framework, followed by fine-tuning through multiple iterations.

In verbal communications, we don't have that luxury. Live editing would be awkward to say the least. Imagine a conversation with real-time verbal editing:

"Hi, Bill, I just read your idea, and I can tell you it won't work."

"I mean, let me say that differently."

"Hello, Bill, I hope you're doing well! Regarding that proposal. Take my word for it. I've been there, done that, and *yikes!*"

"Hold on, let me try that again."

"Hi, Bill, I'm glad to have a chance to chat with you about your idea. I was involved with something similar in the past and . . ."

Honestly, if I were Bill, I would never take another call upon seeing that person's caller ID on my screen!

All humor aside, this is one of the stark differences between verbal and written communications. Taking just a few seconds to carefully craft the verbal message that you wish to convey can result in a striking difference in how you are perceived, and ultimately received, as a respected communicator.

Here is a method to consider that can strengthen your communication effectiveness, drawn from the fundamentals of journalism.

The journalism template builds upon four discrete segments to clearly communicate a message. Consider using these touchpoint objectives when crafting a verbal message. They represent the infrastructure of every news story you hear. The four segments are:

- ▶ **Reportage.** Just the facts
- ▶ **Analysis.** What it means
- ▶ **Commentary.** Thoughts and opinions
- ▶ **Editorialization.** Advocacy

Reportage is all about precision of the facts and details. In essence, the who, what, when, and where only. The "why" kicks in at the analysis stage. As this relates to the workplace, the "why" encompasses details of the business issue or problem being addressed.

Analysis requires the journalist to inform the audience about what the information means. This stage draws inference from the reportage stage regarding meaning, relevance, value, and probable impact. Most importantly, it is based on objectivity and does not push any personal agenda. In the workplace, this translates into giving balanced, fair viewpoints, strictly based on facts or what can be quantified.

Commentary is about opinion and perspective. This stage bridges into the personal opinion of the value and impact. The workplace application here is that it represents the communicator's thoughts and opinions.

Editorialization states your personal recommendations. In the world of media, it is synonymous to telling people what they should do. In the workplace, it is the equivalent. In other words, it's telling others what they should do and why.

The journalistic template serves as a structural platform for communicating a business message. Any of the four components can be used independently, or in combination, to present one's ideas, views, or recommendations to accomplish a specific objective.

In a typical team meeting, when a project is being discussed, it's not uncommon for people to move quickly to the editorial stage. They find themselves pushing their opinions and viewpoints. Unwittingly, they move to advocating their editorialized recommendations. They have strong opinions and promote them. These editorialized statements frequently begin with "I think we should..." or "I have a better idea ..."

This style of forceful advocacy is a contributing factor to meetings taking more time than is necessary. Consider instead applying the journalistic template:

- ▶ State the facts, the condition, the problem (reportage).
- ▶ Express the true meaning, impact, or relevance (analysis).
- ▶ Share personal thoughts, opinions, value for this effort (commentary).
- ▶ Offer perspective, impact; summarize specific action, solution, benefits (editorialization).

Applying the journalistic technique and framework for crafting your message will help ensure your message is received with clarity and respect.

Never Seek to "Win" over the Pursuit of Truth

It cannot be stressed enough—as an evolved leader, it is essential to avoid falling into the destructive and instinctive behavior of wanting to win over pursuing truth.

Our egos can cause us to be quite destructive. Egos can make us defensive and stand in the way of logic and reason. In simple terms, our egos can make us quite stupid—at least functionally.

When we engage in a debate with someone whose opinions are contrary to our own, regardless of what the person might present, we tend to defend our original position without logically evaluating the legitimacy of the opposing view.

Elected officials notoriously operate in this way to the extreme. They will go down in flames defending their party's position. It's almost indistinguishable from a sporting event. If I'm wearing my team's jersey, there is nothing the opposing side can do to sway my allegiance or even recognize when the opposing team achieved something admirable. No one enjoys having to say, "I was wrong," or in a business setting, "My idea isn't as good as yours." We're afraid that doing so lessens our value or suggests we're not smart.

The list of blind, illogical allegiance behaviors is endless. We defend our position with great vigor in an effort to protect our self-image. This destructive practice is the antithesis of how an evolved leader should think and operate. You have the judicial authority to impose a gag order on your ego. Do so, often, and focus entirely on the pursuit of truth.

Maslow's hierarchy of needs confirms that protection of our ego is deeply rooted in instinctive Neanderthal behavior. There's nothing that expresses better how difficult it is to suspend our ego than the aphorism "Easier said than done." To invoke the words of the great Princess Elsa, "Let it go!"—ego, that is.

The path toward the pursuit of truth requires the processing of all available information. It is through active listening that we most productively achieve that goal. Advance the natural evolutionary flow, and push intellect front and center as the primary method for an evolved leader to seek truth.

ACTIVE LISTENING

Great communicators go beyond effectively transmitting their ideas. They ensure their message has been accurately received and understood. But simply confirming that other people understand you is only part of the equation. We must also ensure that we fully comprehend and process their message, as well. Unfortunately, this is something that happens far less frequently than we might think. We believe we've spoken clearly, and unless the other person is incompetent, they would surely have understood what we said.

Active listening is the ongoing cycle of transmitting a message, confirming it has been understood, and requiring acceptance or rejection of that message. The process involves managing two channels. First, is the responsibility to openly receive, accurately understand, and process the information you hear and respond with substantive commentary.

The second channel is the higher-level skill of guiding others, sometimes in the moment, to confirm that their understanding of your message is what you intended to convey. Building skills of active listening must include proficiency of both these channels.

There's the old adage about having two ears and one mouth. It implies people should listen twice as much as they speak. Ratios aside, those who are skilled at active listening don't merely listen well; the listening portion of their conversations will almost always dominate.

Active listening enables you to shape a far more effective strategy. When presenting an idea or brainstorming with a team, applying this skill helps fuel the process of reaching the best solution. At its foundation, active listening is about asking the right questions. The skill of asking the right questions in the right sequence, with synergistic follow-up, provides a powerful advantage.

An entire field of philosophy revolves around Socrates. I've often dreamed of having Socrates alongside me when fielding tough questions from a group of savvy detractors. Let's briefly look at an overview of how the process works.

Channel one of active listening seeks to demonstrate your interest in understanding what has been said. When you hear someone express an idea, or take a position that is counter to yours, ensure that your first response ends with a question mark. This could be as basic as the old standard, "What I understood you to say was . . . . Is that right?"

A more challenging question might be, "What's the upside, and what are the risks in doing it that way?"

The response will, no doubt, further clarify the core message.

Not surprisingly, people are likely to spout the benefits of their ideas but have probably not given careful thought to the risks. Asking someone to discuss the risks, and of course, how they would get around them, is not an act of aggression or a putdown. It is a reasonable business question and always provides more clarity.

Note, the tenor and direction of the discussion will change if the person is unable to cite any risks. This is your opportunity to present any risks you may see and challenge the person to offer solutions.

Channel two of active listening seeks to make the other person an active listener as it relates to your message. The Socratic approach applies here too. When a person opposes an idea you've presented, rather than mounting a defense, ask one of the following questions:

- ▶ "What portion of the idea I've suggested would work?"
- ▶ "What changes to the idea would you suggest to make it more effective?"

A central objective for confirming this is to listen for reaction and feedback. When these are not forthcoming, the evolved leader actively solicits those responses. In doing so, one must manage the very difficult task of remaining open, neutral, and nondefensive—applying the skills of active listening.

In addition to using active listening and the journalistic template to frame your message, an effective communicator uses visceral techniques in delivering the message. It is a method that draws the listener in by creating visual imagery. These reference points foster a sentient reaction to the message, thereby creating a resonant connection to both the story and the speaker. This is commonly known as "charisma."

CHARISMA

It is important to note that although well-structured communication skills support one's charisma, not every good communicator is necessarily charismatic. Although difficult to articulate, we have all experienced being in a group setting where someone walks into the room and exudes an aura of esteem and respect. You can't help but hear the overture "O Fortuna" from Carl Orff's *Carmina Burana*.

Whether it's the inspiring images in Martin Luther King Jr.'s "I Have a Dream" speech, John Winthrop's "City upon a Hill," or Maya Angelou's "Caged Bird," the use of visceral imagery is a technique that engages an audience. Listeners are unaware of being drawn in by this tractor beam. Some charismatic speakers are not necessarily conscious of doing this, as it just comes naturally. Nonetheless, it fuels the charismatic impact.

I remember my dad would step into a room of strangers and instantly capture the attention and admiration of all those who caught his gaze. His unspoken carriage of subtle motions, facial expressions, hand gestures, and confident gait silently spoke volumes. If asked, people would not have been able to put their finger on it, but the effect of engagement and connection was experienced by nearly everyone present.

How does this happen? Are we subtly taught by those who nurture us what to look for in order to make this happen? Or is it simply embedded in nature's DNA? Our social antennae, through both instinct and nurture, enable us to detect a wide range of micromessages. We don't think of them with any more consciousness than the act of raising the corners of our mouth to smile or furrowing our brow to express confusion.

An infant has the natural ability to detect the difference between a casual gaze of curiosity and engagement versus a threatening, aggressive leer. For the most part, it's not taught. It's built into our observational DNA across all cultures.

That old adage "First impressions are lasting impressions" asserts a powerful force. The knee-jerk reaction that causes a first impression has the power to push aside logic and reason. I've encountered many people who, after being presented with facts that invalidate their position, will respond defensively with some version of "Don't try to confuse me with the facts. I know what I feel." It's the age-old problem of allowing our emotions and feelings to supersede logic and reason.

We see what we seek. Once an opinion is reached about someone, instinctive confirmation bias kicks in. Unwittingly, we look for behaviors that confirm what we believe to be true, while at the same time filtering out behaviors that suggest our impression may have been wrong.

In the workplace, when the first impression others have of you is positive, your subsequent behaviors will either reinforce that impression or cause its erosion. However, when an initial impression is negative, the uphill battle to change that opinion becomes much more difficult.

Unfortunately, the amount of effort required to change someone's opinion upward or downward is not equal. It's much easier to fall from the grace of a good first impression than it is to successfully overcome a negative first impression.

Your mission should be to demonstrate behaviors that result in others having a positive first impression regarding you and your leadership skills and impact. Otherwise, it becomes a formidable challenge to regain that respect against the near indelible backdrop of first impressions.

First impressions are sometimes established even before one enters the room via preceding credentials or reputation. An intern attending a strategy meeting among a group of seasoned professionals may have a great solution to a problem being discussed, but that great idea is often overlooked because of its source.

Influencing factors that cause us to reach judgmental first impressions include both profile descriptors and behavioral factors.

It's often said you can't have a great idea in a law firm if you haven't passed the bar, and you can't have a great idea at an engineering company without an engineering degree.

Some of the influencing factors that cause us to reach these judgmental first impressions include both profile descriptors and behavioral factors. Profile descriptors include gender, sex, race, age, size, nationality, and more. Behavioral factors can include speech patterns, gestures, facial expressions, mannerisms, vocabulary, message content, professional and academic credentials, reputation, and more. But here's the rub—even using all these factors, our first impressions often get it wrong.

Charisma is an influential factors that when executed well, will shine a spotlight and can propel upward opportunities for advancement.

Dos and Don'ts of Charismatic Leadership

Here are some specific and actionable behaviors and skills you can apply. These will provide the fuel to create and sustain first impressions others form about you.

First, we'll distinguish the difference between carriage and charisma. Although closely aligned, carriage speaks more to the physical and visual behaviors, while charisma is more about words, tone, content, style, cadence, and other forms of expression.

Carriage Skills

▶ On the carriage side, the first thing people tend to notice is your facial expression. It's not just about the proverbial pleasant smile. It's about not looking morose, angry, cold, or foreboding.

▶ Leaders who are renowned for their charisma often demonstrate the following behaviors. Consider these as you develop your skills of leadership charisma.

• Smile in a way that is reserved and pleasant but not exaggerated or specious.

• Walk using deliberate and extended strides versus clipped, choppy, small steps.

• Maintain a straight but not rigid posture, and avoid looking down.

• Scan the venue with a slow sweep of the room, keeping your head uplifted to convey confidence. Randomly stop and establish visual connection with various members of the group.

• Ensure that your facial expression does not seem tentative. Avoid the deer-in-the-headlights look.

• Laugh when something is genuinely humorous but never out of obligation or politeness. Failing to do this well leaves the impression of one who is easily amused and less urbane.

• Tune your demeanor to reflect genuine engagement, not polite, placid indifference.

▶ Hand gestures, though not consciously thought about, play a major role in the ways we assess a person's stature. Here is a list of don'ts and one, all encompassing, DO for gesturing:

Don'ts

• Don't point at people, only at data and images.

• Don't raise your hands with open forward palms to suggest someone should stop speaking.

- Avoid using the karate chop motion to emphasize your speaking points. You may impress Mr. Miyagi, but it is distracting and creates a negative impression.
- Avoid the church-steeple hand position, placing all five fingers of one hand against the corresponding fingers of the other. Lifting them creates a steeplelike image. Some body language experts suggest that the hand steeple position conveys a sense of confidence and inner strength. More sophisticated observers may see this gesture as cliché or contrived.
- Avoid perpetual nodding to convey understanding or agreement. It signals a lack of judicious thinking.

Do

- Avoid *all* the Don'ts!

At the core, a charismatic person exudes charm, confidence, and a captivating magnetism, all accomplished with an undertone of humility. In essence, the charismatic person makes people feel at ease, respected, valued, equitably engaged, and motivated. They master the skills of carriage.

Charisma is extraordinarily difficult to define with precision or actionable clarity. As Supreme Court Justice Potter Stewart famously said in his 1964 ruling on the definition of obscenity, "I can't define it, but I know it when I see it."

Oddly, charisma is a skill that is virtually never addressed in anyone's performance review or personal development plan. Though not normally verbalized, it may be one of the most powerful skills that enable people to ascend the ranks of higher leadership.

One senior executive who particularly stands out as a model of mastering the art of charisma and carriage is Doug McMillon, CEO of Walmart. He is renowned both within and outside the company for this quality. Working extensively at the company in their Bentonville headquarters, I had the opportunity to meet with him on a number of occasions. Upon our first encounter, it became clear why McMillon has this reputation.

Upon being first introduced, his smile, gestures, expressions, words and tone instantly telegraphed a sense of likability, comfort, and respect.

I recall something, in particular, he did during our first meeting that on the surface might appear minor but became a clear indicator of why people at the company admire his leadership.

I was presenting to his team and casually showed a photo of a prominent figure whose gestures subtlety conveyed a message of defensiveness. As I moved on to the next topic, McMillon stopped me and said, "This is interesting. Would you mind going back and telling me more about what that photo reveals? I'd really like to learn more about that."

On the surface, his query had nothing directly to do with the operations of the world's largest brick-and-mortar retailer. McMillon, however, was intrigued as he saw such subtle messages as one of the core elements of effective leadership. These are the ways we build loyalty, engagement, motivation, and commitment. It wasn't an isolated event. It continued in all subsequent encounters and emails I have exchanged with him since.

Charisma is about what we say, how we say it, and the timing of when we say it. These are some key attributes and techniques that manifest leadership charisma.

Tone

Contrary to what one might expect, charismatic leaders do not constrain their tone of delivery to meet conventional expectations. In general, people often osmose into unaffected styles and tones that enable them to fit in but not stand out.

The tone of an evolved leader needs to stand out as an exception to the norm. Charisma is rarely achieved by one who speaks in scriptlike monotones. Standing out among the crowd requires something other than standard speech patterns. But not all standing out behaviors make you outstanding. Metering and cultural judgment play a critical role; after all, not everything that makes us stand out is outstanding. Effective use of tone varies based on culture, and therefore being the exception will manifest differently. In the military, a commanding, even condescending, tone can be effective. In an environment that operates with the discipline of taking orders and doing what you are told, stripes give rights.

> **My stars and bars never act as fences keeping challenging perspectives at bay.**
> —James Amos, four-star general,
> former US Marine Corps, Commandant

Yet James Amos, the four-star general and former commandant of the US Marine Corps, did not speak in the predictable command-and-control style. Instead, his tone was noticeably different. He used a deep, almost soothing, measured resonance that distinguished his presence and drew people in.

He shattered one of my long-held images of military culture. After spending several hours with him and other multistar Marine generals, I disclosed my rather naïve view of military culture. I had long thought that command and control universally defined their culture. He explained, "That process is certainly a cultural expectation, and even requirement, on the battlefield, but in training environments or in meetings of strategy development, my stars and bars never act as fences keeping challenging perspectives at bay. The decisions I make are often the reflection of honest, candid input I receive and encourage from those who report to me and others as well."

Martin Luther King Jr. used an iconic oratorical style of speech characterized by quavering and tremolo touches to his words. Although effective on the global stage, that same style in a workplace setting might not generate the same positive result.

Strive for having a style that makes you stand out, not for the sake of standing out, but for effectively engaging and drawing people in, setting you apart from the norm. The venue and context drive what works and doesn't work. Although Martin Luther King could never use that style of communicating in a financial firm. His tone and charisma event delivered with vacuous amphigory, would have a captivating impact on a public audience.

Words

Charismatic leaders tend to use words that are uplifting and motivational. Their words convey confidence and strength but also vulnerability. One critical aspect of this skill is a consistent use of open-ended questions. Therapy sessions conducted by any licensed professional are dominated by open-ended questions that drive effective self-analysis and introspection. The value in this approach is not limited to psychotherapy. Being a great leader is not about giving the answers. It's about inspiring others to reach the solutions while getting there through your guidance.

Another key attribute is the avoidance of sarcasm. The effort to be affable and humorous has a good chance of backfiring. Making someone the butt of your joke can *make you* one. Leaders must take great care when using humor as a part of their public speaking. Words that might appear as a safe stroll on the humor beach could have you stepping in quicksand.

Charismatic leaders use language that carries a consistent undertone of being respectful and fair. Sarcasm, facetiousness, and condescension are the polar opposites of those behaviors.

Eye Contact

Another characteristic of admired leaders is the conscious way they make eye contact when speaking and listening. Engagement and connection are largely conveyed through the eyes. Great leaders make everyone feel they are being spoken to personally, no matter how large the crowd. Over hundreds of years, these expressions may go back as far as Biblical scripture and still rings true: "The eyes are the windows to the soul."

Independent of your mouth, your eyes can smile—make them! Eyes communicate a wide range of emotions. They express fear when wide open, dreamy eyes convey love and affection, while squinted eyes communicate anger or disgust. A raised eyebrow can say, "Yes, I agree," or "That's intriguing!" or "You're out of your damn mind!"

Take care you don't allow them to speak without your permission.

Optimism

Although exceptions exist, people are drawn to those with an optimistic aura. This is a defining element of a charismatic personality. Optimism inspires and motivates people to follow you. No matter how dark or difficult the challenge, optimism is what lifts people out of the funk and fog to inspire hope and action.

**Realism can always include optimism.
Charismatic leaders achieve this mash-up.**

Optimism conveys positivity and the hope that inspires commitment. People like being made to feel good. This does not imply one should behave disingenuously. You don't have to pretend being optimistic when conditions appear bleak. The expression "Every cloud has a silver lining" may seem a cliché, but it does carry an effective message for redirecting our attention to more positive and productive goals. Realism can always include optimism. Charismatic leaders achieve this mash-up.

I recall driving a dear friend to the train station after a holiday visit. We arrived more than an hour ahead of her scheduled departure. With no TSA security or baggage check-in requirements, we arrived with a tremendous amount of time to kill and no place to sit. She felt guilty for requesting that we head to the station so early and said, "I know what you're thinking. I'm an overly nervous traveler, and this is taking a lot of time out of your workday."

It was a great opportunity to share my philosophy on optimism. I told her my thoughts didn't go to that dark side at all. My focus was entirely on wanting to find a solution that responded to her need for peace of mind with an early arrival at the station.

I suggested she blow away that dark-cloud interpretation and instead focus on enjoying the extra time we had there at the station. It is always a waste of valuable time and energy to wallow in one's error or misjudgment. The effort should be shifted to making a bad judgment productive for future decision-making. We can't fix today, but we can plan better for the next time. On her next visit, I was quite firm about managing an appropriate lead time for her train's departure. This is not about seeing the glasses as half full versus half empty. The true optimist focuses on how best to manage the water, whatever amount it is.

SENSE OF HUMOR

It is well known that having a good sense of humor is a positive attribute. Humor puts people at ease and lowers their defenses. This is not to suggest that one should strive to create a comedy club atmosphere. That can lower one's leadership aura.

The goal is to create an upbeat atmosphere that facilitates engagement and openness to dialogue. A well-metered, judicious sense of humor can trigger the limbic system and put people at ease.

When people are asked to list the core values they would like to see in their organization, "fun" consistently finds its way high on that list. As an evolved leader, maintain a workplace that is serious but always includes a culture that welcomes and appreciates humor and is not always on the lookout for the boss's dorsal fin.

PERSUASIVENESS

When I ask executives to describe the most important skills necessary for great leadership, persuasiveness always makes its way into the top 10 attributes.

Let me pull no punches here. Being persuasive, as a team leader, may be one of the worst skills to exhibit.

The skill of persuasion is valuable when advocating for project funding, staffing, and a variety of operational needs. If one is a lawyer, being persuasive in negotiating contracts or representing a client in a courtroom is essential. Certainly, in sales or marketing, this skill is an absolute requirement. But as a team leader, leveraging the skill of persuasion can be destructive or even hazardous. I deem persuasiveness as one of the *worst* skills when performing the role of the team leader.

Let's break it down. Assume you're the boss. You wake up in the morning with what you believe is a great idea to move a team project forward. You're also highly skilled at persuasiveness. What is likely to happen when you present your great idea at your next team meeting using your excellent skills of persuasion? There aren't many rhetorical questions in this book, but this is certainly one of them!

Clearly, everyone is going to go along with the boss's idea. But why?

This is the result of either fear or buy-in. When it is fear, it's about not crossing the boss. Actions taken due to fear are about self-protection and in no way are connected to persuasiveness. Persuasion is about *convincing* others to buy into an idea because one is glib and manipulative. Using the power dynamic of persuasion is merely a form of coercion.

Note that I didn't say you would force your idea upon them. People are quite aware when they are being bullied and will either push back or be too fearful and simply go along—but they have not been persuaded.

When someone has strong skills of persuasion, those on the receiving side don't perceive that they are being manipulated or coerced. The person sending the message is just effective at selling the idea and getting others to nod approvingly and ultimately to buy into it. Silver-tongued glibness should be the last reason people support an idea.

Once the boss takes a strong position on anything, his or her subordinates are likely to either acquiesce or be hesitant to push back with opposition. This is not to suggest that people are always obsequious and kiss the "ring" of the leader.

Your colleagues were all hired because of their thinking capacity. They all passed the company's rigorous vetting and hiring process because of this strength. None of them were hired because of their big muscles or good looks. Again, they occupy their seat at the table because of their great minds. How could you ever consider yourself a great leader if you don't tap into those thinking minds for perspective and insight, unpersuaded by the leader's views?

In my interview with Mark Bertolini, former CEO of Aetna, we discussed the dangers of persuasion as a leader.

"We used to think a Harvard or other Ivy League MBA was the best credential for the future CEO of a company. I would now argue exactly the opposite," Bertolini said. "I came out of Cornell believing I had all the right answers and all the right skills. I would go to meetings wondering how long it was going to take people to figure out the answer I already knew. I used to sit and formulate leading questions to try and get people to the answer what I knew was the 'right' one.

"Finally, I had a boss who said to me, 'Why don't you actually listen to the answers for those questions before you conclude what the right answer is—and actually come up with two or three additional questions, based on those alternative responses offered by your team? Maybe you'll learn something new.

"When I first graduated from business school, I thought I had 100 percent of the right answers all the time—I now believe I have the right answer less than 50 percent of the time."

A sign of great leadership is not allowing your ego to interfere with personal growth. Although a brilliant thinker and graduate of Cornell University, Bertolini had the wisdom and vision to make a fundamental shift in the way he listened and processed the thoughts and opinions of his colleagues. I have found this is a rare but admirable skill. People who know they are smart often find it difficult to allow their thinking to be changed by those without matching academic stripes.

> You must allow yourself to be vulnerable enough
> to work together collectively in a group
> to come up with the best answers.
> —Mark Bertolini, former CEO, Aetna

Bertolini continued, "You have to come to your job as you are with all of your successes and failures. And all the baggage of who you are as a human being. You must allow yourself to be vulnerable enough to work together collectively in a group to come up with the best answers."

Be a great idea catalyst, and avoid the heavy hand of persuasiveness that only creates an environment of yes-people. Evolved leaders never persuade or convince people; they solicit perspective and input from others. They neutrally present a concept and solicit input before making a final decision.

CREATIVITY AND INNOVATION

Earlier in the book, creativity and innovation were listed among the high-functioning skills of evolved leaders. In this chapter, let's take a look at another dimension of this skill set.

What does it take to be creative? Isn't creativity just something you're born with—sort of like a sense of humor or temperament? Can it be developed? Once again, the answer is an unequivocal yes!

Creativity is not a mechanical skill, like learning computer coding or writing a business letter, but it can be taught and developed.

At a future staff meeting, consider conducting the following exercises to develop creative thinking skills within your team.

Exercise: Harnessing Creativity

Bring a simple object into the room, such as a bowl, a paper clip, or a shoelace.

Ask each team member to think of three ways the selected object could be used for purposes other than for which it was originally designed. Direct people's answers to fall within the following two categories:

1. Conventional use (other than its originally designed purpose)
2. Highly inventive or unconventional use

For example, the conventional use of a bowl is to hold things like food, loose change, and a myriad of other objects. Not much creative skill required here, just simple recall. An alternative but still conventional use might be as a guide for cutting hair or drawing a circle.

An example of a highly inventive, unconventional use might be to break the bowl into pieces and use them as cutting or digging tools. Another might be to glue the pieces onto a canvas as artwork, reminiscent of the great American contemporary artist Julian Schnabel. His work combines paint on canvas with fragments of kitchenware (bowls, cups, saucers) glued directly onto the canvas, creating an illusionary image emerging from the fragments of broken tableware.[1]

If you view Schnabel's paintings, I'll bet you'll never think of a bowl in the same mundane, utilitarian way again. More importantly, with each exercise, team members' creative thinking will likely expand, not only about the objects they used when doing these exercises, but in the new ways they view work projects and processes.

When first introduced to this exercise, participants may find it difficult to come up with inventive solutions. After just a few rounds, team members will gradually find it far easier to tap into their creative minds. This exercise stimulates ongoing creative thinking.

In the entertainment world, a popular program that aired for seven years in the mid-1980s was *MacGyver*. Angus MacGyver was a secret agent who refused to carry a gun but fortunately never needed one. He relied on his vast practical knowledge of science and powerful creativity skills to make use of anything around him to create solutions to every problem he encountered. Although colloquially used for decades to mean having a knack for inventive problem solving, the name of the program's eponymous protagonist (MacGyver) has since become a dictionary verb and noun in the Oxford and Merriam-Webster dictionaries.

While building creativity skills using these exercises may not make everyone on the team clever enough to use a paperclip to diffuse a nuclear bomb or to deflect a laser beam with binoculars, this approach to building aptitude for creative problem solving, inventiveness, and innovation will certainly be strengthened.

Exercise: Expanding Workplace Creative Vision

Ask team members to think of a topic about which they have little or no functional knowledge or expertise but have a deep intellectual curiosity. One personal example is my fascination with the building of tunnels. How are engineers able to cut a 50-foot-wide opening 100 feet below the surface, under a riverbed, and build concrete walls without the structure collapsing? What an amazing marvel of engineering! It's comparable to the mystery of navigating eight reindeer to every child's home between bedtime and sunrise!

In truth, the tunnels hold greater fascination because I drive through them and witness their marvel every day!

How was this mystery used in a creativity-building exercise? One of my early managers was quite skilled in building team member creative thinking. He asked the members of the team to submit a topic for which they had intellectual curiosity but had no direct application to their current job. No shock here—I went with the tunnel.

Considering that the work demands on employees made it impractical to allocate time for research, the manager assigned this task to an intern to develop a brief presentation on one of the topics every few weeks.

A plethora of benefits arose. The intern developed his business presentation skills through the creation of visuals to unravel the mystery. He also developed his skill to address challenging questions from the members of the group, while building a closer sense of camaraderie with them.

I finally got an answer to my burning question about the mystery of tunnels, and a side benefit to the company was the connection I deepened with the company culture. Boy, did I enjoy working at that company! Small things can make personal connections and can forge loyalty, engagement, and commitment.

Most importantly, months later, someone was discussing a work challenge and referred to something discussed in the tunnel exercise. She said, "The reason this project keeps falling apart is because we don't have someone acting as a 'barrel vault' for reinforcement. We're being delusional if we expect it to work without recognizing this." Everyone got it. That tunnel construction metaphor was the manifestation of our expanded thinking in ways to examine the complexities of a problem.

Obviously, neither the unconventional uses of a bowl nor an exploration of tunnel engineering directly correlate to your team's work projects. But they do nurture and expand creative thinking, which can lead to all sorts of business breakthroughs and benefits.

The important question to ask throughout the work process is, what have we missed? Keep asking that question, and keep people thinking creatively to fuel innovative thinking.

Innovation—Creativity's Counterpart

Innovation is what bridges creative thought with value and application. Mark Zuckerberg's success didn't just come from the creative idea of posting and sharing pictures or locating old friends. His creative concept shifted to innovation when he gave it structure and made it work by bringing value and purpose. The innovation grew further with the incorporation of advertising, news, and creative algorithms that connected the dots between people, interests, and sharing.

The Winklevoss twins, Cameron and Tyler, were the creative masters who invented the original Facebook prototype, HarvardConnection, later named ConnectU. The twins launched their creative platform in 2002.

It remained mostly stagnant and siloed until Mark Zuckerberg stepped in with the innovation to create a strategic marketing plan that transformed its mission and changed the world. His innovative thinking brought powerful value and purpose to the Winklevoss twins' creative concept, transforming it into a major advertising, news, and social media platform. Zuckerberg took it from ideation (creativity) to actualization (innovation.)

Creativity represents a cadre of ideas and imaginative concepts. All too often, they remain in a siloed and stagnant state. Innovation moves it from concept to creative application, effectively addressing the question, what can we do with it and how do we make it viable?

How does the evolved leader develop a team's innovation skills? Here are some questions to pose for every creative idea your team conceives:

- ▶ "Who would want it?"
- ▶ "How would they use it?"
- ▶ "How will it improve their lives or work process?"
- ▶ "Is there something it would replace?"
- ▶ "Does the need for it exist, or does the need have to be created?"
- ▶ "How can it be effectively positioned?"
- ▶ "What is the value and life span?"

In my conversation with Jennifer Zatorski, global managing director of strategic initiatives in the CEO's office of Christie's auction house, we discussed the top skills she values in a leader. She said, "I look for someone who demonstrates the skills of being innovative and a visionary. I want to know if they will bring the business forward by challenging my way of thinking. Next, I look for a high EQ [emotional quotient]. Are they able to build teams and bring out the best in people to work optimally?"

Zatorski shared that the prestigious Christie's auction house is atypical, as the employee base is predominantly female. At her level, however, top leadership is mostly male. It was especially interesting to realize that even in companies that have a counterbalance of gender, that the women at the top encounter many of the same experiences regardless of gender demographics of the larger population. I can't imagine Zatorski being affected by gender matters in any culture, as she is the epitome of charisma.

Regarding innovation and emotional intelligence, she noted, "Being able to identify EQ skills is hard within the confines of an interview, but we always press to uncover these skills because they are a necessary complement to our focus on innovation at Christie's."

It's understandable that EQ skills would be highly valued at Christie's, as its employees are surrounded by some of the world's finest art and artifacts of global culture every day. Leadership in this culture demands extraordinary EQ skills.

> I look for someone who demonstrates the skills of being innovative and a visionary. I want to know if they will bring the business forward by challenging my way of thinking.
> —Jennifer Zatorski, global managing director of strategic initiatives, office of the CEO, Christie's

Among the many senior executives I've met, Jenn Zatorski exuded such high EQ that if I were ever to reenter the corporate world, she is someone I would be proud to work with.

FUTURE DIRECTION

Building diverse teams, managing the hybrid workplace, minimizing proximity bias, managing quiet quitting, powering down, and dealing with the Great Resignation exodus are all workplace conditions that will continue to evolve and require the skills of an evolved leader to execute well.

How does an evolved leader manage the dynamic shift of culture? One pretext is the acceptance that one doesn't typically solve new problems with old tools. In the next chapter, we'll look at some new tools to raise leadership effectiveness that enable you to meet these new demands.

CHAPTER 12

10 Actions for Inclusive Leadership

The 10 Actions for Inclusive Leadership are designed to provide clear, actionable behaviors and a unique set of skills tuned to the upward arc of cultural evolution.

This upward direction is about initiating versus the more standard approaches of remediation. In other words, the evolved leader prevents issues from happening rather than fixing them once they occur. Instead of focusing on cleaning up existing conflicts that seep through the cracks, the evolved leader practices preemptive interactions using the 10 Actions for Inclusive Leadership.

The 10 Actions for Inclusive Leadership tool is a composite of additional new skills and expansion of some of the key points introduced in previous chapters.

These are everyday workplace actions you can apply that generate bursts of progress on both the inclusion and performance fronts and can be easily woven into daily interactions.

Let's explore each of the 10 Actions for Inclusive Leadership (Figure 12.1) to bring you to the next level of preemptive, proactive, and preventive leadership.

THE 10 ACTIONS

1. Balanced Interactions	In staff meetings, with whom do I interact with most? How do my interactions with individuals differ and why?
2. Building Commitment	What specifically do I do to motivate and inspire each team member's engagement?
3. Performance Feedback	How often do I catch team members "doing things right" versus "doing things wrong"?
4. Value Protocols	Do I set procedural and operational standards for my team to support an equitable culture of performance?
5. Business Alignment	Do I conduct quarterly round table discussions with my team on the topic of diversity and inclusion?
6. Interviewing	When interviewing candidates, to what degree does my personal style influence hiring decisions?
7. Team Building	Do I assign choice projects to the same "best" person, or do I develop others to become "best" people?
8. Micromessaging	How do my personal feelings about people influence my gestures, expressions, and tone of voice when interacting with them?
9. Leadership Development	Do I regularly give team members the assignment to facilitate and lead in staff meetings?
10. Managing Challenge	When my viewpoints are challenged, do I respond defensively and justify my position, or do I begin by asking questions that explore the opposing viewpoint?

FIGURE 12.1   10 Actions for Inclusive Leadership

1. BALANCED INTERACTIONS

During staff meetings, we may inadvertently interact with some colleagues more than others, in both frequency and quality through the use of connective language. This can send the subtle message that the contributions of some team members are more valued, important, or respected than others.

This does not suggest that every idea is an effective solution. Rather, every contribution deserves equitable assessment and consideration.

Action

During the course of a meeting, take a mental note of how frequently you interact with different members of your team. At the end of the meeting, reflect on how balanced your interactions were across the group.

Don't default to the inertia of your comfort zone.

Repeat this process over the course of a few meetings. If there is an occasional imbalance, this does not present an issue. If your interactions consistently reveal a disproportionate balance toward some team members than others, take the step toward becoming more inclusive, and direct your responses to counter the imbalance by providing more frequent and comprehensive responses across the team. It is not hard. The investment is minimal, but the returns are invaluable.

Example

You have determined that the majority of your interactions have been directed toward two specific team members. You may feel this is because they are the strongest contributors on the team and provide the best perspective and insight. Although this may be true, you can build a stronger base of emerging talent and competence—don't default to the inertia of your comfort zone. An inclusive leader consciously develops others to ascend to higher levels of competency.

Benefits/Outcomes
Uncovering your unconscious biases of singling out some team members for interactions over others will enable you to refocus and establish a more equitable balance of interactions.

2. BUILDING COMMITMENT

Building commitment is a central skill of great leadership but is never achieved when only done for a select few. Commitment is best achieved when people are motivated and inspired by their colleagues and bosses and how they experience workplace culture.

As the leader, you play a pivotal role in shaping these experiences. The following action provides techniques for building a culture of engagement where team member ideas and contributions are heard, valued, and respected. This is a cornerstone of inclusive leadership.

Action
While conducting one-on-one meetings, make an effort to uncover that person's professional aspirations and any aspects of the job for which he or she is less enthusiastic. These questions take a slightly different approach to those highlighted in stay interviews and can open a window to identify turnover risks.

Example
Consider uncovering this information by asking the following questions:

- ▶ "If you could create your job from the ground up, how would it be different?"

> ▶ "Is there an area outside of your current responsibilities that you would like to learn more about?"
> ▶ "What part of your current job do you value the most/the least?"

Asking probative questions like these powers a process of positive engagement with the employee and builds a solid foundation of respect, which, in turn, fuels commitment, inspiration, and motivation.

Be creative and look for ways to incorporate the information gleaned from the discussion to better align the employee's interests and aspirations with the work assigned.

Benefits/Outcomes

It's been well established that people don't leave companies—they leave bosses and cultures. Building commitment can be a highly effective method for generating enthusiasm, respect, and the belief that their boss has their best interests in mind.

3. PERFORMANCE FEEDBACK

Delivering balanced and developmental feedback is a cornerstone of inclusive leadership. Providing rich and actionable feedback enables others to perform to their potential. Doing it well builds a strong foundation of current and future talent for your team and the entire organization. The inclusive leader ensures that feedback is delivered comprehensively, regardless of the nature of your relationship with someone.

When delivered well, feedback addresses two distinct aspects of an individual's professional development:

1. Technical skills
2. Perception elements

Technical skills include the fundamentals of one's job performance as delineated in the job description and as necessary to carry out assigned duties. Often, these are activities that can be measured against a specific and objective set of standards, such as meeting deadlines, completing work assignments, and having a skill set that involves subject-matter expertise.

Perception elements include a wide range of subjective criteria, such as opinions about someone's ability to collaborate and get along with others, as well as opinions about the person's general attitude and potential for advancement.

This category can be emotionally sensitive, as it is uncomfortable to give or receive feedback regarding how people perceive you, particularly in matters that don't relate directly to the execution of the job. Perception elements are as important as one's technical ability because they influence one's job opportunities and professional advancement.

Action/Examples

Let's look at some suggested techniques for delivering feedback in both categories.

Technical Skills—Feedback

Avoid waiting for designated or official time frames, such as annual performance reviews or the completion of major projects, to provide technical feedback. Feedback about job performance should be provided whenever you interact with someone on a project. This could even be a daily process. Ensure that the feedback is done *equitably* and *consistently* for all team members.

Let's say you've just completed some work on a project with an employee. Take a moment to conduct a brief review and assess the work that was completed. You might ask:

"If you were to give yourself a rating for how you handled this task, what would it be?"

This should be no more than a 5- to 10-minute discussion. Listen carefully to the employee's rating and justification, and then provide your assessment and the rationale behind it. Keep records of your discussions, and use these in compiling that person's annual review.

Take special care to be objective, focusing entirely on actual performance and not sentiment or feelings. In other words, avoid statements like:

- "I was surprised that you . . ."
- "It was disappointing that you . . ."
- "I thought you understood . . ."

Feelings should not be a part of providing objective feedback.

Perception Elements—Feedback

Unlike technical feedback, this should be less frequent and be carefully orchestrated.

Keep uppermost in your mind that due to the sensitive nature of this topic, it is always more effective to get the recipient to sanction your candor before giving this type of feedback. Also, this category of feedback should exclude any comments about one's personal profile, things that cannot be changed, or components of the person's core values.

Using the explanations provided earlier, begin the conversation by describing the two distinct categories of performance feedback to be covered: technical skills and perception elements.

Make it clear that everyone on the team will receive or has already received the same dual spectrum of performance feedback. This will neutralize any concern an individual may have of being singled out and treated differently than others.

To begin your perception feedback, speak directly to the issues, using this sequence of steps:

- Category of concern
- Perceived issue
- Examples
- Recommended action

Example

One could say: "Let's turn to the topic of your perception feedback. The perception falls in the category of commitment. There is a perception you aren't fully engaged and committed to some of the projects you work on.

"For instance, when you delivered your report to Bill, your message seemed cold, disconnected, and obligatory and left the impression of indifference to the value of the work.

"Some recommended actions you might consider for dispelling those perceptions could be to verbally offer some comments and personal perspectives about the content of the report."

This brief model is a template to help guide your discussion. Your actual conversation should be framed based on the responses you get and the advice imparted to support the employee's personal development.

Ensure the employee understands that the perception elements will *not* be a part of their formal performance review unless these elements are specifically outlined in the employee's job description. Instead, stress that the perception elements are part of the employee's developmental counseling and are meant to provide advice to support his or her personal development and advancement opportunities.

Benefits/Outcomes

People look to their managers to help guide and direct their careers. When this is done well, leaders are admired and respected. When people know you have their best interests in mind, it will undoubtedly raise their level of commitment, loyalty, and overall engagement.

At a higher level, providing balanced feedback across your entire group builds a high-performance culture and team.

4. VALUE PROTOCOLS

Value protocols are a critical component of evolved leadership and merited their own chapter earlier in this book. I won't restate all the details here, but it must include the practice that follows. It is an essential part of the 10 Actions for Inclusive Leadership tool.

Establish your own set of value protocols and share them with your team. Let me share my personal favorite: *Require every criticism to include a recommendation.*

It is easy to find fault. Make it your business requirement that any and every time someone offers a criticism, it must be accompanied with a proposed solution. It doesn't have to be the right solution but does minimize the knee-jerk habit of directionless complaining. This value protocol represents a mindset of forward, productive thinking.

Require every criticism to include a recommendation.

Benefits/Outcomes

Providing your team with a set of value protocols fuels more balanced engagement and solutions from not just some but all members of the team.

5. BUSINESS ALIGNMENT

An effective way to demonstrate one's commitment to inclusion is to actively align DEI with routine business. Make DEI an agenda item for a regularly scheduled staff meeting two to three times a year. This can be done as a round table team discussion.

The round table segment should be 20 to 30 minutes. For those that may raise the question on the appropriateness of "wokeness," remind them what "woke in the workplace" actually means. Its objective has nothing to do with political ideologies and external "social justice" issues. It is simply about ensuring that everyone in the workplace experiences a culture that enables them to perform without restrictions, based on their immutable profiles.

Some suggested topics for your roundtable discussion are detailed in the "Example" section that follows.

Action
Provide the specific discussion topic, and ask that people come prepared to share their thinking.

Example
Consider sending a link to a current DEI article in advance of your meeting, as a prereading assignment.

Ask the members of the team their reactions to the article.

Your round table discussion should not be limited to the content of the article alone but include broader DEI topics and perspectives as they may relate to the company in general.

Consider inviting representatives from a few of your company's ERGs to give a brief update on their activities. Encourage an open discussion Q&A on their business objectives. Close the discussion by asking for recommendations that can be forwarded to senior management to improve this area of corporate culture. Should any sensitive issues emerge, be sure to forward these to your designated HR representative.

Benefits/Outcomes
DEI can never achieve the success desired unless people can see its business value. When the business value is widely recognized and DEI is aligned with business operations, the behaviors that support it become more embraced and not obligatory.

6. INTERVIEWING

Job interviews are quite similar to first dates. Both parties come together, in person or virtually, with the objective of determining whether they should or could have an ongoing relationship.

Interestingly, we tend to spend more time with business associates than we do with spouses and partners.

This action step provides perspective and new tactics to widen your recruitment net for capturing the best talent and building a more inclusive team. The primary objective of a job interview is to determine whether it's a "right fit." This means determining whether the candidate has the right skills to perform the assigned tasks, is committed to work for the company to their highest levels, and will be respected by colleagues and respectful toward those they work with.

For the job interview, there should be a consistent set of questions applied for every candidate, and the responses given should be evaluated using the same set of criteria.

Most seasoned interviewers perform this process reasonably well when it comes to assessing a candidate's technical skills. The shortfall tends to arise when the interviewer assesses subjective elements of a candidate's profile and unconsciously, and illogically, allows this information to influence the hiring decision.

> **We mistakenly use a mirror when we should be using a microscope to determine the best talent.**

The inclusive leader separates technical qualifications from the cultural and subjective elements. These lines are easily blurred, causing a person's overall candidacy to be determined by personal compatibility/incompatibility with the interviewer's style preferences versus the objective elements of technical ability and potential to perform well.

An imbalance of these two input channels, technical skills and personal comfort, can become a major obstacle that erodes the goals of inclusion in the hiring process.

A well-executed interview never defaults to the personal comfort or subjective elements. The focus on objective technical skills should, of course, always be the primary filter we use in assessing the quality of one's candidacy.

Remember: don't rely on your emotional gut—instead, go with your brain.

Those gut feelings are primarily fed by looking for our reflection in others. We mistakenly use a mirror when we should be using a microscope to determine the best talent.

Action

One of the biggest missteps is failing to break the habit of allowing personal comfort to dominate your selection process. Don't look for personal compatibility—look for professional capability.

Our natural tendencies draw us to candidates who think like us, behave like us, and, all too often, look like us. For many, the relationships we form in the workplace are extensions of our social values. The decisions of who we bring into our teams should not use the same criteria we apply when we choose our friends or personal relationships.

Eliminate the unconscious practice of placing value on candidates because they fit in. Instead, look for people who are fit—where "fit" means being capable, skilled, and innovative and able to bring a broad set of perspectives to the team.

Example

Use situational questions. Situational questions are structured to pose realistic job scenarios designed to assess a candidate's skills for working through actual job challenges. These could be questions such as:

▶ "You've been given the responsibility to complete the following project [describe project]. How would you begin, and what would be the specific steps along the way to complete it?"

Situational questions can also be applied in retrospect, such as:

> ▶ "Describe a project in your current job—without, of course, revealing confidential information—where you took a project from start to completion and how you managed the obstacles you encountered."

Your assessment of the answer should examine the logic and thoroughness of the response and not whether it resembles what you would do.

Look into any inconsistencies you might observe, and challenge the candidate to explain and resolve them. If you find yourself particularly comfortable with a candidate, this could be a sign of slipping into the "fit-in" trap. Assess what's causing that perception of comfort and whether it's rooted in professional or personal comfort.

Benefits/Outcomes

Building a diverse team has far greater value than the mere formation of a cultural mosaic. A diverse team is the jewel with many facets of different perspectives. It is your role to polish each of the facets so they shine brilliantly.

An ancillary benefit of a demographically diverse workplace is how it acts as a magnet for drawing in innovative talent who want to be a part of a forward-thinking workplace.

7. TEAM BUILDING

What is team building, and why is it important to inclusive leadership?

Team building is the ongoing process of establishing mutual loyalty, commitment, engagement, and support to achieve maximum team performance. The process rests on two separate, interdependent pillars:

▶ Mechanical actions
▶ Psychological status

Combined, they represent the ongoing endeavor to optimize collaborative performance.

Mechanical actions include sourcing the best talent, providing the necessary resources, clarifying team member roles, setting performance expectations, and providing the necessary infrastructure to enable team members to succeed.

Psychological status includes building commitment, loyalty, camaraderie among team members, the desire and willingness to go above and beyond, supporting others to succeed. This is a cornerstone of inclusive leadership because mutual commitment, loyalty, and engagement can never exist without team members feeling respected, valued, and treated equitably.

In the routine course of business, it is not uncommon to assign critical or sensitive projects to those who can be most relied upon to get the job done best. This is usually done with the desire to serve the client and achieve the highest-level results. The intentions are good, supported by the belief that the person selected is best skilled to achieve this outcome.

A risky pattern often emerges when a manager consistently assigns the most desirable projects to the same few go-to people on the team. When those people leave the team or company, the manager is faced with an immediate deficit of developed and skilled resources.

More importantly, this habit of narrow selection fails to live up to the expectations of what is, indisputably, the profile of an admired leader.

Action: Recognition

Although it is common to formally recognize performance associated with high-profile projects, begin to equitably shine the spotlight on high performance from other project areas, as well.

During a meeting, when someone who is less frequently recognized makes a comment of value, you might say:

▶ "Did everyone hear what [name] said? That was a really good point."

- ▸ "Thanks [name], I wouldn't have thought of that idea."
- ▸ "I'm glad you challenged me on that."

Comments like these convey to everyone on your team that you recognize and value their contributions.

Example: Stretch Assignments

Assign special projects to all members of the team, not just your go-to people. Take people out of their comfort zone and expose them to new opportunities that build their skills.

For instance, assign someone to read an article from an industry publication on new findings, techniques, or research that provides new insight to the business. Have the person compile a brief report to present to the team, raising everyone's skill level and showcasing that team member.

Benefits/Outcomes

Leaders who convey an interest in recognizing day-to-day contributions and performance across all team members will develop a tightly knit, mutually supportive, high-performance team.

8. MICROMESSAGING

Inclusive leaders understand the critical distinction between unconscious bias and micromessaging. Applying this knowledge effectively builds loyalty, commitment, engagement, and performance.

> **The science of what defines unconscious bias is interesting, but science doesn't change culture—actions do.**

One key distinction is that unconscious bias is intangible. It is a state of mind. Unconscious bias represents feelings, opinions, conclusions, and judgments. The important realization is that opinions and judgments are not actions.

On the other hand, micromessages are entirely tangible. They are the real-time manifestations of those opinions, thoughts, and judgments from our unconscious bias.

An evolved leader must redirect his or her attention to focus on what can be done in tangible, manageable, controllable, or actionable ways.

To achieve meaningful change, inclusive leaders focus more on the *tangible* and *actionable* manifestations and less on their mental source or the science of bias. The science of what defines unconscious bias is interesting, but science doesn't change culture—actions do.

Action

The meaning of a message is seldom reflected in the words themselves. It is conveyed entirely through the connotations of our micromessages. They are tone of voice, eye contact, nuance, gestures, facial expressions, syntax, and more. These are the micromessages that convey how people come to understand not only what is being conveyed, but whether they are being respected, treated equitably, and valued as a member of the team.

Benefits/Outcomes

Micromessaging is represented through many topical areas in this book and is the foundation for how evolved leaders communicate to enable others to perform to their potential.

9. LEADERSHIP DEVELOPMENT

Although it is important to develop team members' skills to execute their specific assignments, inclusive leaders go a step further. They develop higher-level skills that enable all team members to grow and increase their future potential.

Action

Select a team member for whom you'd like to provide targeted development. Select a topic for which that person will be responsible for leading the discussion in an upcoming team meeting.

Example

Let's say the topic you assign is "Project Budget." Meet with the employee and provide guidance on how to lead the discussion. Here are some discussion points you might consider assigning:

▶ Poll the group on their individual budget status.

▶ Solicit discussion on any shortfalls and, if there are, discuss the details.

▶ Determine whether the current budget is adequate to meet future needs.

▶ Take the team's pulse to prioritize the most, and least, critical expense items.

▶ Have the team members identify what items they would eliminate if budget cuts are required.

▶ Discuss other items needed to reach the topic resolution.

Following the meeting, conduct a debrief to assess the employee's opinion about how effectively he or she completed the task. Use this opportunity to provide balanced feedback and development.

Benefits/Outcomes

Completing this item not only develops and broadens an employee's skills but allows the employee to be seen through a different set of lenses by colleagues. Every employee on the team should be given the opportunity to take on these types of developmental roles as a routine part of modeling inclusive developmental leadership.

10. MANAGING CHALLENGE

Reigning in our ego has been a consistent theme throughout this text. It rears its ugly head in more instances than one might imagine—people don't want to be wrong, particularly in the presence of those who report to them.

Those who welcome challenge are often viewed with greater admiration than those who take a defensive stance.

Defensiveness steps in as a shield to protect one's ego. We've talked about how that "defensiveness" shield can be better managed when the challenge is directed toward you.

The evolved leader must also have the skill to mediate when heated challenges arise among team members. As the leader, it is your responsibility to be the guiding voice to manage the discourse.

As long as team members continue gripping their shields in a combative stance, it is impossible to reach the most objective and logical solutions.

Action

Never allow your or others' egos interfere with the pursuit of truth. Guide your team toward the value protocol, "Every challenge should be respectfully vetted for its merit before reaching any conclusion." When your ideas or strategies are challenged, consider the following inclusive leadership approaches.

Example

Here are some recommended approaches to manage defensive or even combative exchanges:

- ▶ Ask those holding adversarial positions to stop and describe what the other person is advocating. Then have that person confirm that the understanding was accurate and if not, explain the delta.
- ▶ Ask those holding opposing views whether any parts of the other's ideas have merit.

These actions act as "reset" and redirect the discussion into a more productive channel.

Benefits/Outcomes

Conflicts among team members is not an uncommon occurrence. When these conflicts occur, the team is not only operating in an inefficient manner, but the drive for each to be victorious means the most influential contender, and his or her ideas, wins—not necessarily the idea that offers the best solution.

IMPLEMENTING THE 10 ACTIONS FOR INCLUSIVE LEADERSHIP

Each of these 10 Actions for Inclusive Leadership can be executed at any time. They don't link to or follow any prescribed workplace behavior issues, and they don't need to be activated in any particular order. If implemented consistently, they will help build loyalty, engagement, and commitment to foster an inclusive business culture.

Do We Really Need Leaders at All?

The significant problems we face cannot be solved
at the same level of thinking we were at when we
created them. They certainly won't be solved by one
person even, and especially, the one at the top.

—ALBERT EINSTEIN

The arc of change spanning the existence of humankind is elegantly and simply expressed by the geometric equation $y = 2^x$, where y is the workplace and x represents time.

The graphic representation (Figure E-1) begins at approximately a 45-degree angle and turns upward exponentially. When we consider there has been more technological advancement in the past century than in all the time preceding, it's hard to imagine where the workplace will be in just the next decade or two.

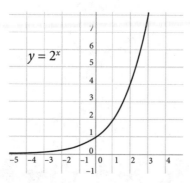

FIGURE E-1   The Arc of Change

Given the pace of change, it's foolish to assume that over the next century the workplace will have any semblance of the construct we operate within today. I recall the stories my parents shared that defined the workplace of their youth at that time. Most people worked with their hands. There were few desk jobs. My father worked as a laborer in a shipyard. That work culture was a strict, command-and-control environment. The boss told people what to do. No questions were asked. People complied and completed their tasks. People knew their place and stayed there. New ideas and innovation never came from the rank and file. They only flowed from the top down.

Many of the workplace constraints were driven by gender, race, and other dimensions that were considered legitimate criteria for determining positions, promotions, and salary differences. The only time employees played a role in change was when it involved safety. Even then, it was voiced through their unions. "Collaboration" was only a word in the dictionary.

Evolution has already placed us at a vastly higher point on that graph than that antiquated era. The velocity of change is breathtaking.

It's a jarring thought that within the next half century the sophisticated thinking of today will seem just as "ancient" through the eyes of our future leaders—*if we have leaders at all.*

Yes, at the heart of this trajectory is the question, will the workplace need leaders at all in the not so distant future? There is a high probability the answer will be no—at least in the way we define the role of a leader today. A multitude of models have been imagined by futurists. Here is one I feel has great promise.

WEBSPHERE OF AUTOGENOUS INTERDEPENDENCIES

The WebSphere of Autogenous Interdependencies (WAID) is a self-correcting, self-improving, interconnected autonomous system that along with ongoing advances in artificial intelligence will likely vanquish our current leadership and organizational models (Figure E-2).

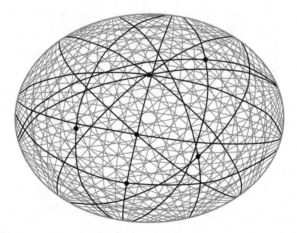

FIGURE E-2 WebSphere Model

Spiders weave intricate and delicate webs. This interconnected system enables them to instantly identify anything that threatens the web's integrity. From any position along its strands, the arachnid detects the size and location of the disruption from a foreign object;

and in a fraction of a second, it attacks, disables, and consumes and repairs any damage to the web.

Similarly, the WAID leadership model, by the very nature of its construct, includes a sensitivity tuned to detect anything that disrupts the WebSphere's operating system from any point of contact, disruption, or need within its interconnected system.

Imagine a WAID workplace with the intelligence and power to design, construct, diagnose, repair, and monitor its interdependent operational efficiency, collaboratively, through the nanotechnology with little or no human interaction.

Technology is already moving in this direction. Several self-configuring robotic systems like this have emerged and are operational today. AI systems are now able to monitor, diagnose, and repair any intervention that disrupts the well-being and efficiency of its process. These systems also have the capability to learn from mistakes or any damage inflicted from the interventions and to build structures that prevent future threats.

In one example, T. Tomiyama and H. Yoshikawa, in the article "Systems for Image Forming Apparatus," describe a plurality of sensors interfacing with a system control circuit that aligns to a case memory segment and work script memory system. Although more technically complex than I'll ever understand, it represents a fully functioning, self-diagnostic and self-repair system and structure.

Our own internal systems function somewhat similarly. In human biology, internal maintenance depends upon an autonomous internal system able to identify internal and external threats and dispatch the necessary curative response. No thought process is required for the body to identify the threat and initiate repair. In fact, much of the repair and maintenance happens in our sleep.

The system works independently of our consciousness. Although controlled by the brain, there is no conscious involvement. I am the chairman of the board of my brain, but my consciousness doesn't have a vote.

No consciousness is involved when jogging and instructions are given to my heart to beat faster and pump more blood. There is no executive command issued to my lungs to expand and contract more rapidly while on that jog. This internal WAID-type system takes control.

In the human body, these functions are controlled by a highly sensitized WebSphere-like process. They work in quiet concert to maximize the body's efficiency and health.

Autonomous, self-healing AI systems have figured out how to create the interdependent web without calling a meeting or sending an email. It's not unfathomable that the future leadership model could mimic this highly sophisticated WAID.

In ways that may be a foretelling of this future state, many companies operate today with a high degree of organizational autonomy and a culture of "leading at all levels," engaging people to contribute their intellect and energy to solving their companies' toughest business challenges.

In these forward-thinking organizations, colleagues who have virtually no real-time contact, and work in disparate time zones, design, manage, produce, and distribute complex products. All functions along the burgeoning WebSphere can easily identify when a lapse may have occurred and inject their expertise in the repair or production process. If additional expertise is needed, they can connect the network to other resources that support and ensure success.

The present-day leadership pyramid model bestows the power of decision-making upon a single senior executive who reigns supreme at the peak of the pyramid. That person and the senior executives are granted divisional power based on business disciplines. They then utilize that power to cascade their vision through their respective organizations.

As the pyramid descends, employee count increases while decision-making power decreases. This structure flows counter to the fundamentals of logic that suggest those who are closest to a problem have a better perspective on the obstacles that inhibit or enable a solution.

Notwithstanding the great value that those closest to the problem can provide for maximizing efficiency, it cannot be ignored that futuristic vision comes from a different skill set. When Jeff Bezos was the CEO of Amazon, he didn't need to have direct contact with the mechanisms that run the complex warehousing and distribution systems to create the future vision of the company. The combination of both technical and functional astuteness, along with creative and innovative thinking, maximizes the process of futuristic visioning.

The WAID model acts as the emulsifier, as in science, that enables particles to mix and become a suspension of both elements, but not dissolve. Each component retains its autonomy, but the interdependencies of the components work in unison with the other parts of the suspension—but they remain functionally immiscible.

Here's how it might work. Under the traditional structure, when a client experiences a flaw with a device, it is brought to the area with technical expertise for its repair. The repair is executed, and the customer leaves satisfied. The underlying cause for the malfunction is often not identified or fed back into the business intelligence.

With WAID, the underlying cause of the malfunction is monitored, and an assessment is made to determine whether the repaired component performs better or worse than the original. Modifications to circumvent future malfunctions are forwarded to R&D, as well as to other interconnected areas that maximize business efficiency and performance.

When the volume or seriousness of the problem reaches the magnitude for a spotlight to be shone on it, other business entities engage. A classic example is an auto manufacturer's recall. Particularly noteworthy is that recalls, in general, involve matters of health and safety. Failure to uncover the problem subjects the business to potentially devastating legal exposure and risk.

A future state, without formal leaders, could instantly detect such problems and both raise efficiency and lower costs.

WAID supports a philosophy that the exchange of information should be ubiquitous throughout the organization and not limited to risk prevention—an approach that certainly enables more timely solutions to identified problems. The WAID structure circumvents the many layers and labyrinths of obstacles found within traditional organizational models that typically prevent rapid solutions. With WAID, when the need for repair is signaled through its self-diagnostic system, all related areas are instantly pinged. Details that are pertinent to all the discrete areas in the company are instantly connected through this WAID.

When patterns emerge, decisions regarding how to address them are made among those immediately responsible for the specific work to be done. This is not unlike the way advanced security systems work in the monitoring and prevention of terrorist threats—connecting the dots and their interdependencies. This is not something our governments have the expertise to develop. Think tanks, defense contractors, and other experts have developed these systems to monitor the trillions of web touches at any given moment, share the web touches with each node of their WebSpheres, and then analyze them for a possible threat and response.

Our look at one possible transformation of the leadership model may represent a long-term evolution, changing everything about what defines organizational leadership. Whether that path takes us toward WAID or some other yet to be envisioned direction, there is certainly no question that what our leadership model will become in the future will have only a semblance of what we are comfortable or familiar with today.

There is no reason our future won't be able to emerge and evolve into this unknown operational, interdependent autonomy—*provided that the WebSphere doesn't take humans out of the equation altogether!*

Regardless of the accuracy of any predictions of the future, change is happening at warp speed. It is essential that our models of leadership evolve to meet the demands of the unseen future.

LEADING INTO THE FUTURE

We've described a wide range of leadership behaviors that together can help create an evolving culture that enables all the company's human talent to perform to their full potential. Evolved leaders put these concepts and skills into practice. They move from ideological concepts to practical application, with culture taking center stage.

As we noted, research reveals that toxic culture is now the leading reason people leave their jobs. In this environment, more and more responsibility falls on leaders to build enabling cultures that support peak performance and engagement. The mission of evolved leaders is to go beyond eliminating toxicity and strive to implement the skills and behaviors provided in this book.

From setting the stage for developing new skills, to managing our workplace persona differently than our personal selves, to focusing more on outcomes than humility, to seeking truth over feeding our egos and saving face, to using Socratic instead of instructive methodologies for conflict resolution, to giving priority to logic and reason over emotion and gut feelings, to infusing value protocols as personal operating principles—all of these will elevate you to reach beyond the mere mechanical approaches that define transformational leadership. Set your goals to attain the more lasting and authentic impact of being an evolved leader who inspires and motivates the performance of others from the core and leads them into the future.

Notes

CHAPTER 3

1. Jennifer Liu, CNBC, 1/14/2022.
2. *Harvard Business Review*, 3/10/2017.
3. William Arruda, "9 Differences Between Being a Leader and a Manager," *Forbes*, November 15, 2016.

CHAPTER 6

1. https://stateofchildhoodobesity.org/national-obesity-monitor/.

CHAPTER 10

1. "Do You Really Know Why Your Employees Leave Your Company," *Harvard Business Review*, https://hbr.org/2019/07/do-you-really-know-why-employees-leave-your-company.

CHAPTER 11

1. Julian Schnabel, "Number 1 (The Two Fridas)," https://airmail.news/arts-intel/events/julian-schnabel-self-portraits-of-others-4810.

Index

About the Author

Stephen Young is the Senior Partner of Insight Education Systems, a management consulting firm specializing in leadership and organizational development services. As a recognized leader and foremost expert in this field, Mr. Young frequently consults with and provides executive coaching for senior executives and management teams of Fortune 500 companies and businesses, at all levels.

For more than a decade, Steve has been a featured speaker at business conferences worldwide. He is much sought after for his powerful and engaging presentation style. His widely acclaimed seminar MicroInequities: Managing Unconscious Bias™ has been embraced by over 20 percent of Fortune 500 corporations in 35 countries in every region of the world and is touted by corporate leaders as the new paradigm for building effective corporate cultures.

As a featured speaker, Mr. Young delivers his seminar to a wide range of academic institutions, including Harvard Business School, Princeton University, Yale, and MIT.

His work has been published in numerous business articles and recognized in a wide range of business publications, including the *Wall Street Journal, Time Magazine, Harvard Business Review*'s *Management Newsletter,* and throughout the International Press. His program was also featured by Oprah Winfrey in multiple issues of her *O, the Oprah* magazine.

His top-selling book, *Micromessaging: Why Great Leadership Is Beyond Words*, is a McGraw Hill top-selling business classic.

As former Senior Vice President and Chief Diversity Officer at JPMorgan Chase, Mr. Young managed the firm's diversity strategy worldwide. Under his leadership, the company garnered numerous awards for its initiatives, including the Catalyst Award, *Fortune Magazine*'s Top 50 Companies for Minorities Award, the Best Companies Award from *Working Mother Magazine,* and *Diversity Inc Magazine*'s designation as the number one company for DEI.

Prior to joining JPMorgan Chase, Stephen was Vice President for Diversity with Bank of America. He is a former staff member of the Rutgers University Graduate School of Management, served on the Diversity Committee for the United Way of America, served on his local Board of Education, and was an Advisory Board member of Rev. Jesse Jackson's Wall Street Project. He is the former Chairman of the Securities Industry Association's Diversity Committee and was a Board Member of *Scholastic*'s Alliance for Young Writers and Artists. Young is also the author of *Seven Steps to Master the Interview and Get the Job* (Random House) and *How to Manage Time and Set Priorities* (Random House).

He is distinguished for converting conceptual business initiatives and vision into tangible, measurable, and actionable applications.